Portuguese Phrase Book

Portuguese translation and
phonetic transcription by
Teresa de Paiva-Raposo

Portuguese Phrase Book

Edmund Swinglehurst

HAMLYN
LONDON · NEW YORK · SYDNEY · TORONTO

First published in 1981 by
The Hamlyn Publishing Group Limited
London· New York· Sydney· Toronto
Astronaut House, Feltham, Middlesex, England.

ISBN 0 600 37263 4

Set on Linotype VIP System in Portuguese Times
by Tek Typesetting

Printed in Great Britain by
Hazell Watson & Viney Ltd, Aylesbury, Bucks.

Distributed in the U.S. by
Larousse & Co. Inc., 572 Fifth Avenue, New York,
New York 10036.

Contents

Introduction

The Hamlyn Portuguese Phrase Book is designed to help the reader who has no previous knowledge of the language. With its aid he should be able to make himself readily understood on all occasions and to cope with the host of minor problems – and some major ones – that can arise when on holiday or travelling in Portugal and Brazil.

The key to successful speech in a foreign language is pronunciation, and an outline of the principles of vowel and consonant sounds and their usage in Portuguese is to be found at the beginning of this book. This is followed by a section dealing with the essential elements of Portuguese grammar. A close study of these two sections and constant reference to them will be of the utmost value: with the pattern of sentence construction in mind and a feeling for the sound of the language, the reader will be well equipped to use the phrases in this book.

These are set out in logical order, beginning with the various means of travel and entry to the country. The section on accommodation covers the whole range from hotels and private houses and villas to youth hostels and camping sites. Particular attention is paid in the chapter on eating and drinking to the many varieties of Portuguese fish and the selection of famous Portuguese wines. Shopping, too, is covered in detail: whether the reader wishes to buy silver filigree jewellery or to equip his self-catering apartment with a week's supply of groceries, he will find a choice of phrases easy to refer to and simple to use.

Entertainment, sightseeing, public services, and general conversations in the hotel bar are all covered, and there is an important section on looking after your money. In addition to carefully chosen phrases, each section includes an appropriate vocabulary which is as comprehensive as possible, and at the end of the book there are quick-reference metric conversion tables for the more important temperatures, weights and measures and an index to all the phrases.

The Hamlyn Portuguese Phrase Book will not only enable the traveller to handle any situation with confidence but will help to make his stay in Portuguese-speaking countries a more enjoyable one.

Guide to Portuguese Pronunciation

This is intended for people with little or no previous knowledge of Portuguese and is based on English pronunciation, providing an approximate English equivalent for all Portuguese sounds. This means that it is not entirely accurate, but the reader who pays careful attention to this section should be able to follow the phonetic transcription, which is used throughout the book, and thus make himself reasonably well understood in Portuguese.

The Vowels

LETTER	APPROXIMATE PRONUNCIATION	SYMBOL	EXAMPLE
a	between *a* in bat and *a* in rather	ah	**vaso** vahzoo
a, â	like *a* in ago (usually unstressed)	a	**lâmina** lameena
e, é	like *e* in bell	e	**panela** panela
e, ê	like *ea* in pear	eh	**sabonete** saboonehtə
e	1 like *e* in taken (almost silent)	ə	**cabide** kabeedə
	2 like *ee* in bee (when unstressed at the beginning of a word)	ee	**editar** eedeetahr
i	like *ee* in bee or *i* in machine	ee	**vida** veeda

i	like *i* in possible	ə	**ministro** məneeshtroo
o	like *o* in hot	o	**fome** fomə
o, ô	like *aw* in paw	aw	**escova** əshkawva
o	like *o* in root	oo	**comer** koomehr
u	1 generally like *oo* in root	oo	**costume** kooshtoomə
	2 silent when following *g* or *q* before *e* or *i*		**guitarra** geetahrra

Vowel sounds written as two letters

LETTERS	APPROXIMATE PRONUNCIATION	SYMBOL	EXAMPLE
ai	like *y* in by	y	**baile** bylə
au	like *ow* in cow	ow	**cautela** kowtela
ei	like *ay* in day	ay	**leite** laytə
eu	two sounds: like *ea* in pear followed by *oo* in root	ehoo	**ardeu** ardehoo
iu	two sounds: like *ee* in bee followed by *oo* in root	eeoo	**fugiu** foozheeoo
oi	like *oy* in toy	oy	**boi** boy

| ou | like *aw* in paw | aw | **ouvir**
awveer |
| ui | two sounds: like *oo* in root
followed by *ee* in bee | ooee | **ruivo**
rrooeevoo |

Nasal Vowels

A nasal vowel is one with a tilde mark, e.g. **cão,** or a vowel followed by *m* or *n* in certain positions. It is uttered through the nose and mouth at the same time and is pronounced like the vowel followed by *ng*. These two letters are used in the phonetic transcription to represent a nasalized vowel.

LETTERS	APPROXIMATE PRONUNCIATION	SYMBOL	EXAMPLE
ã, am, an	like *a* in ago nasalized	ang	**maçã** masang
em, en	like *ea* in pear nasalized	ehng	**pente** pehngtə
im, in	like *ee* in bee nasalized	eeng	**pintor** peengtawr
õ, om, on	like *aw* in paw nasalized	awng	**apontar** apawngtahr
um, un	like *oo* in root nasalized	oong	**atum** atoong
em (usually at the end of a word or by itself), êm, final en	like *ay* in day nasalized	ayng	**massagem** masahzhayng
êm	like *ay* in day followed by *ea* in pear nasalized	ayehng	**têm** tayehng

ãe, ãi	like *ay* in day nasalized	ayng	**cãibra** kayngbra
ão	like *ow* in cow nasalized	owng	**botão** bootowng
õe	like *oy* in toy nasalized	oyng	**balões** baloyngsh
ui	like *oo* in root followed by *ee* in bee nasalized	ooeeng	**muito** mooeengtoo

The Consonants

LETTER	APPROXIMATE PRONUNCIATION	SYMBOL	EXAMPLE
b	as in English	b	
c	1 like *c* in cat before *a*, *o*, and *u*	k	**carro** kahrroo
	2 like *s* in sit before *e* and *i*	s	**cinto** seengtoo
ç	like *s* in sit	s	**calças** kahlsash
ch	like *sh* in shape	sh	**chuva** shoova
d	as in English	d	
f	as in English	f	
g	1 like *g* in gate before *a*, *o*, and *u*	g	**gato** gahtoo
	2 like *s* in pleasure before *e* and *i*	zh	**girafa** zheerahfa
h	always silent		**hotel** otel

LETTER	APPROXIMATE PRONUNCIATION	SYMBOL	EXAMPLE
j	like *s* in pleasure	zh	**viajar** veeazhahr
l	as in English	l	
lh	like *lli* in million	lly	**batalha** batahllya
m	as in English except when forming part of a nasal sound	m	
n	as in English except when forming part of a nasal sound	n	
nh	like *ni* in onion	ny	**vinho** veenyoo
p	as in English	p	
q	1 like *k* in king	k	**quadro** kooahdroo
	2 when *qu* is followed by *e* or *i* the *u* is silent		**qualquer** kooahlker **máquina** mahkeena
r	1 rolled like the Scottish *r* at the beginning of a word or syllable	rr	**rápido** rrahpeedoo
	2 like *r* in very between vowels or at the end of a word or syllable	r	**pares** pahrəsh **gostar** gooshtahr
rr	rolled like the Scottish *r*	rr	**socorro** sookawrroo

s	1 like *s* in sit at the beginning of a word or after a consonant	s	**sala** sahla **pulseira** poolsayra
	2 between two vowels like *z* in zebra	z	**casa** kahza
	3 like *sh* in shape at the end of a word or before the consonants *c, f, p, q,* and *t*	sh	**mês** mehsh **pasta** pahshta
	4 like *s* in pleasure before a voiced consonant	zh	**asma** ahzhma
ss	like *s* in sit	s	**passar** pasahr
t	as in English	t	
v	as in English	v	
x	1 like *sh* in shape at the beginning of a word, before a consonant and occasionally between two vowels	sh	**xarope** sharopə **excesso** əshesoo **vexame** veshahmə
	2 usually like *s* in sit between two vowels	s	**trouxe** trawsə
	3 like *z* in zebra in initial *ex* before a vowel	z	**exemplo** eezehngploo
	4 like *x* in axe in a number of words derived from Greek and Latin	ks	**sexo** seksoo

LETTER	APPROXIMATE PRONUNCIATION	SYMBOL	EXAMPLE
z	1 like *z* in zebra at the beginning of a word and between two vowels	z	**zero** zeroo **beleza** bəlehza
	2 like *sh* in shape at the end of a word	sh	**luz** loosh

Stress

Words ending in the single unnasalized vowels *a, e,* and *o* and in *m* and *s* are usually stressed on the last syllable but one: **vaso, cautela, origem.**

All other words are usually stressed on the last syllable: **pintor, aqui, maçã, hotel, botão.**

Exceptions to these rules usually have an accent written on the stressed syllable: **rápido, invisível, quiçá.**

In the imitated pronunciation used in this book stress is shown by printing the stressed syllable in bold type.

Can you please help me?	**Pode ajudar-me por favor?** podə azhoodahr-mə poor favawr

Pronunciation of Brazilian Portuguese

The main differences between Brazilian Portuguese (BP) and European Portuguese (EP) lie in vocabulary, grammatical structure (see **A Little Grammar in Action**), spelling and pronunciation. The most important variations in pronunciation are outlined below.

LETTER	PRONUNCIATION	EXAMPLE	PHONETIC TRANSCRIPTION
a	BP usually has an open *a* (ah) where EP has a closed *a* (a)	**aparador**	ahpahrahdawr (BP) aparadawr (EP)
d and t	in BP usually pronounced like *ch* in church when they precede an *i* or an unstressed *e* (ee)	**disse**	cheesee (BP) deesə (EP)
e	1 BP usually has an open *e* (e) at the beginning or in the middle of a word where EP has an almost silent *e* (ə)	**terramoto**	terrahmotoo (BP) tərramotoo (EP)
	2 in BP like *ee* in bee at the end of a word	**conhece**	koonyesee (BP) koonyesə (EP)
	3 in BP *e* is always closed, i.e. pronounced like *ea* in pear, before a nasal consonant	**condenado**	kawngdehnahdoo (BP) kawngdənahdoo (EP)
ei	in BP like *ea* in pear	**primeiro**	preemehroo (BP) preemayroo (EP)
o	in BP like *aw* in paw before a nasal consonant	**comigo**	kawmeegoo (BP) koomeegoo (EP)
ô	in both BP and EP like *aw* in paw, but used much more in BP	**tônico** **tónico**	tawneekoo (BP) toneekoo (EP)
r	in BP usually silent at the end of a word	**parar**	pahrah (BP) parahr (EP)
s	in BP usually like *s* in sit at the end of a word	**baratas**	bahrahtas (BP) barahtash (EP)

A Little Grammar in Action

Nouns

All nouns in Portuguese are either masculine or feminine whether they refer to living beings or inanimate objects. Nouns ending in -*o* are usually masculine and those ending in -*a* are usually feminine. Nouns ending in a consonant or -*e* may be either masculine or feminine.

Before masculine nouns the word for 'the' (or definite article) is **o** and before feminine nouns it is **a**.

o rapaz	the boy	**a casa**	the house
o homem	the man	**a mulher**	the woman
a mãe	the mother		

To form the plural nouns ending in a vowel add -*s* and those ending in a consonant usually add -*es*. The word for 'the' is **os** before masculine plural and **as** before feminine plural nouns.

os rapazes	the boys	**as casas**	the houses

Nouns ending in -*m* drop the *m* and add -*ns* to form the plural.

o homem os homens the men **a nuvem as nuvens** the clouds

Nouns ending in -*l* drop the *l* and add -*is* or -*s* to form the plural.

o lençol os lençóis the sheets **o canil os canís** the kennels

Nouns ending in -*ão* take one of the following plural endings: -*ões*, -*s* or -*ães*.

o balão   os balões   the balloons   a mão   as mãos   the hands   o pão
os pães   the loaves

The word for 'a' (or indefinite article) is   **um**   before a masculine noun
and **uma** before a feminine noun.

um comboio   a train   **uma rapariga**   a girl

The word 'of' showing possession is translated by   **de**   in Portuguese, **de**
and **o** being shortened to **do, de** and **a** to **da, de** and **um** to **dum, de**
and **uma** to **duma**,   etc.

o livro do rapaz   the boy's book
a mãe da mulher   the woman's mother
as portas duma casa   the doors of a house

Adjectives

Adjectives agree in number and gender with the noun they accompany,
that is, they change their endings according to whether the noun is
masculine, feminine or plural. They generally follow the noun. Adjectives
ending in -o change to -a in the feminine.

o rapaz pequeno   the little boy
a casa encarnada   the red house

Adjectives ending in -e and most of those ending in a consonant do not
change in the feminine.

o livro azul   the blue book
a porta azul   the blue door
um homem inteligente   an intelligent man
uma mulher inteligente   an intelligent woman

To form the plural adjectives ending in *-o*, *-a* or *-e* add *-s;* adjectives ending in a consonant add *-es*.

as raparigas bonitas	the pretty girls
os livros ingleses	the English books

To form the comparative and superlative forms put **mais** before the adjective.

um livro caro	an expensive book
um livro mais caro	a more expensive book
o livro mais caro	the most expensive book

Demonstrative Adjectives

The words for 'this' and 'that' are as follows:

este homem	this man	**essa rapariga**	that girl
estes homens	these men	**essas raparigas**	those girls
esta mulher	this woman	**aquele livro**	that book
estas mulheres	these women	**aqueles livros**	those books
esse comboio	that train	**aquela casa**	that house
esses comboios	those trains	**aquelas casas**	those houses

Note. Both **esse** and **aquele** mean 'that' but **aquele** is used of something further away.

Possessive Adjectives

The words for 'my', 'your', 'his', etc. change their form according to whether the noun they refer to is masculine, feminine or plural.

The only exceptions are **dele** ('his', 'her') and **deles, delas** ('their') which refer to the possessor rather than the thing possessed.

	SINGULAR		PLURAL	
	MASC	FEM	MASC	FEM
my	o meu	a minha	os meus	as minhas
your	o teu	a tua	os teus	as tuas
your (pol. form)	o seu	a sua	os seus	as suas
his/her/its	o seu	a sua	os seus	as suas
his	o ..dele	a ..dele	os ..dele	as ..dele
her	o ..dela	a ..dela	os ..dela	as ..dela
our	o nosso	a nossa	os nossos	as nossas
your	o vosso	a vossa	os vossos	as vossas
their	o seu	a sua	os seus	as suas
their (masc.)	o ..deles	a ..deles	os ..deles	as ..deles
their (fem.)	o ..delas	a ..delas	os ..delas	as ..delas

Note that **o teu,** etc. and its plural **o vosso,** etc. are the familiar forms of 'your', used only with members of the family, children and close friends. **O seu,** etc., which is the form of the third person meaning 'his', 'her', 'its' or 'their', is also the normal polite word for 'your' when speaking to all other people.

a minha filha	my daughter
as minhas filhas	my daughters
o teu irmão	your brother
os teus tios	your uncles
o seu pai	your/his/her father
os seus primos	your/his/her cousins
a sua mãe	your/his/her mother
as suas férias	your/his/her holidays
o carro dele	his car
o carro dela	her car
o nosso almoço	our lunch
as nossas coisas	our things
o vosso apartamento	your flat
as vossas casas	your houses
o seu barco	your/their boat
o seus amigos	your/their friends

| a sua casa | your/their house |
| a suas vidas | your/their lives |

| o pais deles | their (masc.) country |
| as roupas delas | their (fem.) clothes |

Personal Pronouns

The words for 'I', 'you', 'he', etc. are as follows:

1 When used as the subject of a verb:

eu	**canto**	I sing
tu	**cantas**	you sing
você	**canta** (pol. form)	you sing
o senhor/a senhora	**canta** (pol. form)	you sing
ele	**canta**	he sings
ela	**canta**	she sings
nós	**cantamos**	we sing
vós	**cantais**	you sing
vocês	**cantam** (pol. form)	you sing
os senhores/as senhoras	**cantam** (pol. form)	you sing
eles	**cantam**	they sing (masc.)
elas	**cantam**	they sing (fem.)

2 When used as the direct object of a verb:

O senhor Pinto vê-me		Mr Pinto sees me
	-te	you
	-o (pol. form)	you (masc.)
	-a (pol. form)	you (fem.)
	-o	him/it
	-a	her/it
	-nos	us
	-vos	you
	-os (pol. form)	you (masc.)
	-as (pol. form)	you (fem.)
	-os	them (masc.)
	-as	them (fem.)

3 When used as the indirect object of verb:

O senhor Pinto diz-me	Mr Pinto says to me
-te	you
-lhe (pol. form)	you
-lhe	him
-lhe	her
-nos	us
-vos	you
-lhes (pol. form)	you
-lhes	them

When used as the direct or indirect object, in European Portuguese pronouns are usually placed after the verb, to which they are joined by a hyphen:

A Maria vende-as	Maria sells them
O João dá-te o anel	João gives you the ring

But in Brazilian Portuguese the pronoun is placed before the verb:

A Maria as vende
João te dá o anel

In European Portuguese the object pronoun is placed before the verb in the following cases.

(a) In negative sentences:

A Maria nunca as vende	Maria never sells them
O João não o tem	João does not have it

(b) After interrogative words:

Como é que a Maria as vende?	How does Maria sell them?
Quando é que o João a vê?	When does João see her?

(c) After prepositions:

Antes de as vender	Before selling them
Para o ver	In order to see him

(d) After conjunctions:

Embora ela as venda	Although she sells them
Enquanto ele o tem	While he has it

(e) In relative clauses:

Ele diz que a Maria as vende	He says that Maria sells them
Ela sabe que o João o tem	She knows that João has it

Note that when a direct and an indirect object pronoun occur together in the same sentence the following contractions are made:

me + o = mo	**O João dá-mo**	João gives it to me
me + a = ma	**dá-ma**	João gives it to me
te + o = to	**dá-to**	João gives it to you
te + a = ta	**dá-ta**	João gives it to you
lhe + o = lho	**dá-lho**	João gives it to you (pol. form), to him, to her
lhe + a = lha	**dá-lha**	João gives it to you (pol. form), to him, to her

me + os = mos	**O João dá-mos**	João gives them to me
me + as = mas	**dá-mas**	João gives them to me
te + os = tos	**dá-tos**	João gives them to you
te + as = tas	**dá-tas**	João gives them to you
lhe + os = lhos	**dá-lhos**	João gives them to you (pol. form), to him, to her
lhe + as = lhas	**dá-lhas**	João gives them to you (pol. form), to him, to her

4 When used after a preposition:

Estes livros são para mim	These books are for me
ti	you
si[você]*	you
(pol. forms)	
ele	him
ela	her
nós	us

Estes livros são para [vocês]*	you
(pol. form)	
eles	them (masc.)
elas	them (fem.)

Combined with the preposition **com**:

O José vai comigo	José is going with me
contigo	you
consigo [com você]*	you
(pol. forms)	
com ele	him
com ela	her
connosco	us
convosco	you
[com vocês]*	you
(pol. form)	
com eles	them (masc.)
com elas	them (fem.)

*Used in Brazil

In Portuguese the polite way of addressing people is to use **o senhor, a senhora** or **você,** when talking to one person and **os senhores, as senhoras** or **vocês** when talking to more than one person. **Tu** is the familiar singular form, and should only be used when speaking to children, relatives and close friends. **Vós,** the plural of **tu,** is no longer in use, so when addressing more than one close friend use **vocês.**

Verbs

The whole subject of Portuguese verbs is too complicated for detailed discussion in a phrase book but for the traveller who wants a quick grasp of verbs with which he can communicate while staying in Portuguese-speaking countries the following basic rules will be useful.

Regular Verbs

Most Portuguese verbs are regular in their formation and fall into one of three categories or conjugations. Note that subject pronouns are usually omitted since the verb endings generally show which person is referred to.

1   Verbs ending in *-ar* in the infinitive.

comprar	to buy
eu compro	I buy
tu compras	you buy
você compra	you buy
ele compra	he buys
/ela	/she
nós compramos	we buy
vocês compram	you buy
eles compram	they buy
/elas	

2   Verbs ending in *-er* in the infinitive.

vender	to sell
eu vendo	I sell
tu vendes	you sell
vocês vende	you sell
ele vende	he sells
/ela	/she
nós vendemos	we sell
vocês vendem	you sell
eles vendem	they sell
/elas	

3   Verbs ending in *-ir* in the infinitive.

partir	to leave, depart
eu parto	I leave
tu partes	you leave
você parte	you leave
ele parte	he leaves
/ela	/she
nós partimos	we leave
vocês partem	you leave
eles partem	they leave
/elas	

To form the negative of a verb **não** is placed before it:

Não vendemos livros	We do not sell books
Não partimos hoje	We are not leaving today

To ask a question it is often sufficient to keep the normal order of words with a different intonation:

Vendem cigarros?   Do you sell cigarettes?

Irregular Verbs

The following are a few of the more useful common irregular verbs.

ser	to be		**estar**	to be
eu sou	I am		**eu estou**	I am
tu és	you are		**tu estás**	you are
você é	you are		**você está**	you are
ele é	he is		**ele está**	he is
/ela	/she		**/ela**	/she
nós somos	we are		**nós estamos**	we are
vocês são	you are		**vocês estão**	you are
eles são	they are		**eles estão**	they are
/elas			**/elas**	

'To be' is translated by **ser** when it describes a permanent condition. It is translated by **estar** when it indicates a temporary state or condition.

O gelo é frio	Ice is cold
Ela é alta	She is tall
Estamos cansados	We are tired

Note that 'there is' and 'there are' are translated by **há,** one of the few forms of the verb **haver** commonly used in modern Portuguese.

Há um cão na casa	There is a dog in the house
Há muitas praias em Portugal	There are many beaches in Portugal

ter	to have		**dizer**	to say
eu tenho	I have		**eu digo**	I say
tu tens	you have		**tu dizes**	you say
você tem	you have		**você diz**	you say
ele tem	he has		**ele diz**	he says
/ela	/she		**/ela**	/she

nós temos	we have	nós dizemos	we say
vocês têm	you have	vocês dizem	you say
eles têm	they have	eles dizem	they say
/elas		/elas	

dar	to give	**fazer**	to make, do
eu dou	I give	eu faço	I make
tu dás	you give	tu fazes	you make
você dá	you give	você faz	you make
ele dá	he gives	ele faz	he makes
/ela	/she	/ela	/she
nós damos	we give	nós fazemos	we make
vocês dão	you give	vocês fazem	you make
eles dão	they give	eles fazem	they make
/elas		/elas	

ir	to go	**poder**	to be able
eu vou	I go	eu posso	I can
tu vais	you go	tu podes	you can
você vai	you go	você pode	you can
ele vai	he goes	ele pode	he can
/ela	/she	/ela	/she
nós vamos	we go	nós podemos	we can
vocês vão	you go	vocês podem	you can
eles vão	they go	eles podem	they can
/elas		/elas	

pôr	to put	**querer**	to want
eu ponho	I put	eu quero	I want
tu pões	you put	tu queres	you want
você põe	you put	você quer	you want
ele põe	he puts	ele quer	he wants
/ela	/she	/ela	/she
nós pomos	we put	nós queremos	we want
vocês põem	you put	vocês querem	you want
eles põem	they put	eles querem	they want
/elas		/elas	

trazer	to bring	**vir**	to come
eu trago	I bring	**eu venho**	I come
tu trazes	you bring	**tu vens**	you come
você traz	you bring	**você vem**	you come
ele traz	he brings	**ele vem**	he comes
/ela	/she	/ela	/she
nós trazemos	we bring	**nós vimos**	we come
vocês trazem	you bring	**vocês vêm**	you come
eles trazem	they bring	**eles vêm**	they come
/elas		/elas	
ver	to see	**saber**	to know
eu vejo	I see	**eu sei**	I know
tu vês	you see	**tu sabes**	you know
você vê	you see	**você sabe**	you know
ele vê	he sees	**ele sabe**	he knows
/ela	/she	/ela	/she
nós vêmos	we see	**nós sabemos**	we know
vocês vêem	you see	**vocês sabem**	you know
eles vêem	they see	**eles sabem**	they know
/elas		/elas	

NOTE. Where a word in Brazilian Portuguese differs from that used in Portugal the Brazilian form is shown in square brackets [ ] in the Phrase Book.

We have missed the train.   **Perdemos o comboio [trem].**

Since in Portuguese the form of a word may change according to gender, as, for example, when the speaker is a woman, this alternative form is occasionally given, in round brackets ( ), in the Phrase Book.

I am asthmatic/diabetic.   **Sou asmático(a)/diabético(a).**

Portuguese Spoken

Portuguese is spoken in Portugal, Madeira, Macao and the Azores. It is also spoken in the countries that were once part of the overseas Portuguese Empire – Timor, Angola, Guinea-Bissau, Mozambique and Brazil.

Portugal

There are two main cities in Portugal, Lisbon and Oporto. As well as these centres of industry, there are many resorts which thrive on the visits of tourists who arrive both in summer and winter.

LISBON is on the River Tagus and is the capital of Portugal. The city is built on flat land surrounding the harbour rising quickly up into seven hills from which there are fine views. In the centre of lower Lisbon, the Baixa, is the Rossio Square and on a hill above it is the older Alfama district, with a castle and picturesque streets. Historic churches, museums, and wide elegant boulevards are some of the attractions of the city.

OPORTO is built on the steep banks of the River Douro and is the centre of the port wine trade. Wine warehouses occupy the Vila Nova de Gaia bank and towards the sea there are handsome villas overlooking the fashionable beach resorts. Three bridges link the river banks.

COIMBRA lies towards the centre of the country. The third largest city, it is the seat of an ancient university and was the first capital of Portugal.

VIANA DO CASTELO is the northernmost seaside resort and grew as a fishing port after the discovery of America. FIGUEIRA DA FOZ is another fishing port and a shipbuilding centre which has sprung into prominence as a holiday resort because of its fine beaches. NAZARÉ, another fishing village and beach resort, attracts tourists because it has retained many traditional customs.

THE ALGARVE in the deep south is a holiday coast with superb beaches and a picturesque coastline where there has been substantial but discreet hotel development. The airport is at FARO, which is also a resort in its own right.

MADEIRA is part of an archipelago and FUNCHAL is the capital of the main island. The island is volcanic and has subtropical vegetation. Its scenery is wild and beautiful and in Funchal one can find good hotels and other holiday attractions.

Brazil

The largest and one of the wealthiest countries in South America, Brazil is largely undeveloped but has modern and beautiful cities on and near the coast. RIO DE JANEIRO and its superb harbour are spectacular and SÃO PAULO equals any of the world's great cities in sophistication and style. BRASILIA, the capital, is a modern city in the interior of the country.

The most exciting event of the Brazilian calendar is the Carnival which begins on the Saturday before Ash Wednesday.

Here to start with are some simple expressions of greeting and leave taking:

Good morning.	**Bom dia.** bawng deea
Good afternoon.	**Boa tarde.** bawa tahrdə
Good evening.	**Boa tarde/Boa noite.** bawa tahrdə/bawa noytə
Good night.	**Boa noite.** bawa noytə
How are you?	**Como está?** kawmoo əshtah
I'm very pleased to meet you.	**Muito prazer.** mooeengtoo prazehr

| How do you do? | **Como está?** |
| | kawmoo əshtah |

| Goodbye. | **Adeus [Até logo].** |
| | adehoosh [ate logoo] |

Some words of courtesy:

| Please. | **Por favor.** |
| | poor favawr |

| Thank you. | **Obrigado (obrigada).** |
| | obreegahdoo (obreegahda) |

| It's very kind of you. | **É muito amável.** |
| | e mooeengtoo amahvel |

| You are welcome. | **Não tem de quê.** |
| | nowng tehng də keh |

| Not at all. | **De nada.** |
| | də nahda |

| I am so sorry. | **Peço imensa desculpa.** |
| | pesoo eemehngsa dəshkoolpa |

| Excuse me. | **Desculpe.** |
| | deshkoolpə |

| It doesn't matter. | **Não faz mal.** |
| | nowng fahsh mahl |

And some questions:

| Do you speak English? | **Fala inglês?** |
| | fahla eengglehsh |

| Where is the hotel? | **Onde é que é o hotel?** |
| | awngde e kə e oo otel |

| What did you say? | **O que é que disse?** |
| | oo kə e kə deesə |

| When does the train leave? | **Quando é que parte o comboio [o trem]?** |
| | kooangdoo e kə pahrtə oo kawngboyoo [oo trayng] |

Who are you?	**Quem é o senhor (a senhora)?** kayng e oo sənyawr (a sənyawra)
How much does it cost?	**Quanto é que custa?** kooangtoo e kə kooshta
How long does it take?	**Quanto tempo demora?** kooangtoo tehngpoo dəmora
Which is the road to ...?	**Qual é a estrada para ...?** kooahl e a əshtrahda para ...
Why are we waiting?	**Porque é que estamos à espera?** poorkə e kə əshtahmoosh ah əshpera

Finally some useful common phrases:

Yes.	**Sim.** seeng
No.	**Não.** nowng
Why?	**Porquê?** poorkeh
How?	**Como?** kawmoo
When?	**Quando?** kooangdoo
What?	**O quê?** oo keh
Where?	**Aonde?** aawngdə
How much?	**Quanto?** kooangtoo
How many?	**Quantos (quantas)?** kooangtoosh (kooangtash)

Please speak slowly.

Por favor fale devagar.
poor favawr fahlə dəvagahr

I do not understand
Portuguese very well.

Não percebo [entendo] muito bem português.
nowng pərsehboo [ehngtehngdoo] mooeengtoo bayng
poortoꝏgehsh

Will you write it down
please?

Escreva se faz favor.
əshkrehva sə fash favawr

How do I say...?

Como é que se diz?
kawmoo e kə sə deesh

What is the meaning
of ...?

O que é que quer dizer ...?
oo kə e kə 'ker deezehr

Please explain how
this works.

Pode explicar como é que isto funciona?
podə əshpleekahr kawmoo e kə eeshtoo foongseeawna

How far is it to ...?

Qual é a distância até ...?
kooahl e a dəshtangseea ate

Where is the nearest
...?

Onde é o ... mais próximo?
awngde e oo ... mysh proseemoo

What time is it?

Que horas são?
kə orash sowng

Will you please help
me?

Pode ajudar-me por favor?
podə azhoodahr-mə poor favawr

Can you point to
where we are on this
map?

Pode-me mostrar onde é que estamos neste mapa?
podə-mə mooshtrahr awngde e kə əshtahmoosh nehshtə
mahpa?

Which way do I go?

Por onde é que eu vou?
poor awngde e kə ehoo vaw?

Is there an official
tourist office here?

Há aqui um centro oficial de turismo?
ah akee oong sehngtroo ofəseeahl də tooreeshmoo

Where is	**Onde é que é**
	awngde e kə e
the station/ bus terminus/ bus stop?	**a estação/o terminal dos autocarros/a paragem do autocarro?**
	a əshtasowng/oo tərmeenahl doosh owtokahrroosh/a parahzhayng doo owtokahrroo
Where do I buy tickets?	**Aonde é que se compra os bilhetes?**
	aawngde e kə sə kawngpra oosh bəllyehtəsh
Am I too early?	**Cheguei cedo demais?**
	shəgay sehdoo dəmysh
It is too late.	**É tarde demais.**
	e tahrdə dəmysh
We have missed the train/bus.	**Perdemos o comboio [trem]/o autocarro [ônibus]**
	perdehmoosh oo kawngboyoo [trayng]/oo owtokahrroo [awneeboos]
Do I turn right/left?	**Viro à direita/à esquerda?**
	veeroo ah deerayta/ah əshkehrda
Do I go straight ahead?	**Sigo em frente?**
	seegoo ayng frehngtə
What is the name of this street?	**Como é que se chama esta rua?**
	kawmoo e kə sə shama eshta rrooa
How do I get to ...?	**·Como é que se vai para ...?**
	kawmoo e kə sə vy para
It is too expensive.	**É caro demais.**
	e kahroo dəmysh
Please give me the change.	**Dê-me o troco por favor.**
	deh-mə oo trawkoo poor favawr
I am tired/hungry/ thirsty.	**Estou cansado/com fome/com sede.**
	əshtaw kangsahdoo/kawng fomə/kawng sehdə

It is very hot/cold.	**Está muito calor/frio.** əshtah mooeengtoo kalawr/freeoo
Please take me to my hotel.	**Leve-me ao hotel por favor.** levə-mə ow otel poor favawr
Is the service included?	**O serviço está incluido?** oo sərveesoo əshtah eengklooeedoo
Thank you very much.	**Muito obrigado (obrigada).** mooeengtoo obreegahdoo (obreegahda)

And some idiomatic expressions:

Go away.	**Vá-se embora.** vah-sə ehngbora
Leave me alone.	**Deixe-me em paz.** dayshə-mə ayng pahsh
Shut up.	**Cale-se.** kahlə-sə
Oh hell!	**Que chatice!** kə shateesə
How goes it?	**Tudo bem?** toodoo bayng
So so.	**Assim, assim.** asseeng asseeng
You're joking.	**Está a gozar.** əshtah a goozahr
Don't move.	**Não se mexa.** nowng sə mehsha
That's it.	**É isso mesmo.** e eessoo mehshmoo

You're right.   **Tem razão.**
                       tehng rrazowng

Carry on.   **Continue.**
                       kawngteenooə

All Aboard

Both road and rail communications in Portugal follow routes either parallel to the coast or out of the coastal towns up the valleys that lead into the mountainous mass of central Spain. The main road from north to south comes from Santiago de Compostela in Spain, crossing the frontier at Valença do Minho on the Minho river. This road then runs through Oporto, Coimbra, Lisbon and south to Lagos in the Algarve.

The types of train in operation are:

TER	Trans-Europe Express (Madrid-Lisbon)
Expresso	a fast stopping train
Rápido	a fast direct train
TAF	an autorail

Car travel in Portugal is slow owing to the hilly terrain and narrow roads. A self-drive car can be useful, though, especially along the Algarve where there are many resorts within a few miles of each other.

In Brazil the roads between main cities are good, but distances are so great that everyone flies. For those who prefer the train the Rio de Janeiro – São Paulo service is excellent and there are also first-class services to Brasilia and Belo Horizonte. For inexpensive travel use the comfortable Brazilian bus network.

Arrivals and Departures

Going through Passport Control and Customs

At the airports and ports there are always people who speak fluent English, but this is not the case at all frontier posts. It is useful, therefore, to know one or two basic phrases. Apart from making communication easier, they help to establish a friendly relationship with officials and often smooth the passage through frontiers.

Good morning/ afternoon/evening.	**Bom dia/boa tarde/boa noite.**
	bawng deea/bawa tahrdə/bawa noytə
Here is my passport/ visitor's card.	**Aqui está o meu passaporte/ cartão de visita.**
	akee əshtah oo mehoo pahsaportə/kartowng də vəzeeta
I am on holiday/on business.	**Estou de férias/em negócios.**
	əshtaw də fereeash/ayng nəgoseeoosh
I am visiting relatives/ friends.	**Vim visitar a minha família/os meus amigos.**
	veeng vəzeetahr a meenya fameeleea/oosh mehoosh ameegoosh
Here is my vaccination certificate.	**Está aqui o meu certificado de vacina.**
	əshtah akee oo mehoo sərtəfeekahdoo də vaseena
The visa is stamped on page...	**O visto está carimbado na página...**
	oo veeshtoo əshtah kareengbahdoo na pahzheena
They did not stamp my passport at the entry port.	**Não carimbaram o meu passaporte no porto de chegada.**
	nowng kareengbahrang oo mehoo pahsaportə noo pawrtoo də shəgahda
Will you please stamp my passport? It will be a souvenir of my holiday.	**Pode carimbar o meu passaporte se faz favor? Será uma lembrança das minhas férias.**
	podə kareengbahr oo mehoo pahsaportə sə fahsh favawr? sərah ooma lehngbrangsa das meenyas fereeash
I will be staying a few days/two weeks/a month.	**Fico uns dias/duas semanas/um mês.**
	feekoo oongsh deeash/dooash səmanash/oong mehsh
I am just passing through.	**Estou só de passagem.**
	eshtaw so də pasahzhayng
My wife and I have a joint passport.	**A minha mulher e eu temos um passaporte em conjunto.**
	a meenya moollyer ee ehoo tehmoosh oong pahsaportə ayng kongzhoongtoo

The children are on my wife's passport.	**As crianças estão registadas no passaporte da minha mulher.**
	ash kreeangsash əshtowng rrəzheeshtahdash noo pahsaportə da meenya moollyer
I didn't realize it had expired.	**Não me dei conta que tinha expirado.**
	nowng mə day kawngta kə teenya əshpeerahdoo
Can I telephone the British Consulate?	**Posso telefonar para o Consulado Britânico?**
	posoo tələfoonahr para oo kawngsoolahdoo breetaneekoo
I have nothing to declare.	**Não tenho nada para declarar.**
	nowng tenyoo nahda para dəklarahr
Do you want me to open my cases? Which one?	**Quer que eu abra as minhas malas? Qual delas?**
	ker kə ehoo ahbra ash meenyash malash? kooahl delash
They are all personal belongings.	**É tudo artigos pessoais.**
	e toodoo arteegoosh pəsooysh
I have a few small gifts for my friends.	**Trago umas lembranças para os meus amigos.**
	trahgoo oomash lehngbrangsash para oosh mehoosh ameegoosh
I have 200 cigarettes, some wine and a bottle of whisky/gin.	**Tenho duzentos cigarros, vinho e uma garrafa de uisque/de gin.**
	tenyoo doozehngtoosh seegahrroosh, veenyoo ee ooma garrafa də ooeeshkə/də zheeng
They are for my personal consumption.	**São para consumo pessoal.**
	sowng para kawngsoomoo pessooahl
Do I have to pay duty?	**Tenho que pagar direitos?**
	tenyoo kə pagahr deeraytoosh
I have no other luggage.	**Não tenho mais bagagem.**
	nowng tenyoo mysh bagahzhayng
Do you want to see my handbag/briefcase?	**Quer ver a minha carteira [bolsa]/pasta?**
	ker vehr a meenya kartayra [bawlsa]/pahshta

I can't find my keys.	**Não encontro as chaves.** nowng ehngkawngtroo ash shahvəsh
I have 800 Escudos in currency, and 8000 Escudos in travellers' cheques.	**Tenho oitocentos escudos em dinheiro e oito mil em travellers' cheques.** tenyoo oytoosehngtoosh əshkoodoosh ayng dənyayroo ee oytoo meel ayng travellers' cheques
I can't afford to pay duty.	**Não tenho dinheiro para pagar os direitos.** nowng tenyoo dənyayroo para pagahr oosh deeraytoosh
Can you keep it in bond?	**Pode guardar no armazém?** podə gooardahr noo ahrmazayng
Here is a list of the souvenirs I have bought.	**Está aqui uma lista das lembranças que comprei.** əshtah akee ooma leeshta dash lehngbrangsash kə kawngpray
You haven't marked my suitcase.	**Não marcou a minha mala.** nowng markaw a meenya mahla
May I leave now?	**Já me posso ir embora?** zhah mə posoo eer ehngbora

At Airports, Terminals and Stations

Where can I find	**Onde é que está** awngde e kə əshtah
a porter?	**um porteiro?** oong poortayroo
a luggage trolley?	**um carrinho?** oong karreenyoo
the left-luggage office?	**o depósito de bagagem?** oo dəpozeetoo də bagahzhayng
my registered luggage?	**a minha bagagem registada?** a meenya bagahzhayng rrəzheeshtahda
That's my case.	**Essa é a minha mala.** esa e a meenya mahla

| There's one piece missing. | **Falta uma mala.** |
| | fahlta ooma mahla |

| That's not mine. | **Isso não e meu.** |
| | eesoo nowng e mehoo |

| Have you seen the representative of my travel company? | **Viu o representante da minha agência de viagens?** |
| | veeoo oo rrəprəzehngtangtə da meenya azhehngseea de veeahzhehngsh |

| Is there an airport bus into town? | **Há um autocarro [ônibus] do aeroporto para a cidade?** |
| | ah oong owtokahrroo [awneeboos] doo eropawrtoo para a seedahdə |

| Where does it go from? | **Onde é o ponto de partida?** |
| | awngde e oo pawngtoo də parteeda |

| Please take my bag to the bus/taxi/car. | **Pode levar a minha mala até ao autocarro/taxi/ carro, por favor.** |
| | podə ləvahr a meenya mahla ate ow owtokarroo/ tahksee/kahrroo poor favawr |

| How much per case? | **Quanto é por cada mala?** |
| | kooangtoo e poor kada mahla |

Toilets

| Is there a ladies' toilet/ gentlemen's toilet? | **Há uma casa de banho para senhoras/para homens?** |
| | ah ooma kahza də banyoo para senyawrash/para omehngsh |

Have you	**Tem**
	tehng
any soap?	**sabonete?**
	saboonehtə
any toilet paper?	**papel higiénico?**
	papel eezhee-eneekoo
a clean towel?	**uma toalha limpa?**
	ooma tooahllya leengpa

a comb or hairbrush?	**um pente ou uma escova?**
	oong **pehng**tə aw ooma əsh**kaw**va
Shall I leave a tip?	**Deixo gorgeta?**
	dayshoo goor**zheh**ta

Telephone

Where are the public telephones?	**Aonde é que são os telefones públicos?**
	aawngde e kə sowng oosh tələ**fon**əsh **poo**bleekoosh
I need a telephone directory.	**Preciso duma lista telefónica.**
	prə**see**zoo **doo**ma **leesh**ta tələfo**nee**ka
Where can I get some change?	**Aonde é que posso arranjar troco?**
	aawngde e kə **po**soo arrang**zhahr traw**koo
Can I dial this number or do I ask the operator?	**Posso ligar este número directamente ou peço à telefonista?**
	posoo lee**gahr ehsh**tə **noom**əroo deeretameh**ng**tə aw **pe**soo ah tələfoo**neesh**ta
Hullo.	**Está?**
	əsh**tah**
May I have Lisbon 12345?	**Liga-me para o um dois três quatro cinco em Lisboa?**
	leega-mə **pa**ra oo oong doysh trehsh **koo**ahtroo **seeng**koo ayng **leesh**bawa
Can I reverse the charges?	**Posso mandar pagar no destino?**
	posso mang**dahr** pa**gahr** noo də**shtee**noo
I want a person-to-person call.	**Quero uma chamada pessoal.**
	keroo ooma sha**mah**da **pe**sooahl
I have been cut off.	**Cortaram-me a chamada.**
	koor**tah**rang-mə a sha**mah**da
You gave me the wrong number.	**Deu-me o numero errado.**
	de**hoo**-mə oo **noom**əroo eer**rah**doo

| May I speak to ...? | **Posso falar com ...?** |
| | posoo falahr kawng |

| Is she not in? | **Ela não está?** |
| | ela nowng əstah |

| Tell her I called. My name is... | **Diga-lhe que eu telefonei. O meu nome é...** |
| | deega-llyə kə ehoo teləfoonay. Oo mehoo nawmə e |

S IGNS

Booking Office	**Balcão de reservas**	bahlkowng də rrəzervash
Coach Station	**Estação de camionetas**	əshtasowng də kameeonetash
Exit	**Saída**	saeeda
Escalator	**Escada rolante**	əshkahda rroolangtə
Information Office	**Informaçoẽs**	eengfoormasoyngsh
Left Luggage	**Depósito de bagagem**	dəpozeetoo də bagahzhayng
Porters	**Porteiros**	poortayroosh
Taxis	**Táxis**	tahkseesh
Toilet	**Casa de banho**	kahza də banyoo
Platform	**Plataforma**	plahtaforma
Underground	**Metropolitano**	mətroopooleetanoo
Waiting Room	**Sala de espera**	sahla də əshpera

Taxi Rank

| Where can I get a taxi? | **Onde é que se apanha um táxi?** |
| | awngde e kə sə apanya oong tahksee |

| Please get me a taxi. | **Arranja-me um táxi por favor?** |
| | arrangzha mə oong tahksee poor favawr |

| Are you free? | **Está livre?** |
| | əshtah leevrə |

| Take me to Avenida da Liberdade. | **Leve-me à Avenida da Liberdade.** |
| | levə-mə ah avəneeda da leebərdahdə |

How much will it cost? | **Quanto é que vai custar?**
kooangtoo e kə vy kooshtahr

That's too much. | **Isso é caro demais.**
eeso e kahroo dəmysh

Turn right/left at the next corner. | **Vire à direita/à esquerda na próxima esquina.**
veerə ah deerayta/ah əshkehrda na proseema əshkeena

Go straight on. | **Siga em frente.**
seega ayng frehngtə

I'll tell you when to stop. | **Eu digo-lhe onde deve parar.**
ehoo deegoo-llyə awngdə devə parahr

I'm in a hurry. | **Estou com pressa.**
əshtaw kawng presa

Take it easy. | **Calma aí!**
kahlma aee

Can you please carry my bags? | **Pode levar as minhas malas se faz favor?**
podə ləvahr ash meenyas mahlash sə fahsh favawr

Newsstand/Kiosk

Have you got English papers or magazines? | **Tem jornais ou revistas inglesas?**
tehng zhoornysh aw rrəveeshtash eengglehzash

Have you any paperbacks? | **Tem livros de bolso?**
tehng leevroosh də bawlsoo

Is there a local paper? | **Há um jornal do local?**
ah oong zhoornahl doo lookahl

Do you sell timetables? | **Vendem horários?**
vehngdayng orahreeoosh

Have you a guide/map to the city? | **Tem um guia/mapa da cidade?**
tehng oong geea/mahpa da seedahdə

Have you   **Tem**
                                  tehng

any writing paper and envelopes? **papel de carta e envelopes?**
                                  papel də **kah**rta ee ehngvəlopəsh

any sellotape?   **fita-cola?**
                                  feeta **ko**la

any matches?   **fósforos?**
                                  foshfooroosh

any cigarettes?   **cigarros?**
                                  see**gahr**roosh

any stamps?   **sêlos?**
                                  sehloosh

a ball-point pen?   **uma esferográfica?**
                                  ooma əshferograh**fee**ka

any string?   **cordel?**
                                  koordel

Information Bureau

Is there an   **Há aqui um centro de informação?**
information bureau   ah a**kee** oong **sehng**troo də eengfoorma**sowng**
here?

Have you any leaflets?   **Tem folhetos?**
                                  tehng foo**llyeh**toosh

Have you a guide to   **Tem um guia de**
                                  tehng oong **geea** də

hotels?   **hoteis?**
                                  o**taysh**

pensions?   **pensões?**
                                  peng**soyngsh**

youth hostels?   **lares de estudantes?**
                                  lahrəsh də əshtoo**dang**təsh

camp sites?   **parques de campismo?**
                                  pahrkəsh də kang**peesh**moo

Do you find accommodation for visitors?	**Tratam de alojamento para turistas?** trahtang de aloozhamehngtoo para tooreeshtash
I want	**Queria** kəreea
a four- or five-star hotel.	**um hotel de quatro ou cinco estrelas.** oong otel də kooahtroo aw seengkoo əshtrehlash
a two- or three-star hotel.	**um hotel de duas ou três estrelas.** oong otel de dooash aw trehsh əshtrehlash
a pension.	**uma pensão.** ooma pengsowng
a single room.	**um quarto de pessoa só (um single).** oong kooahrtoo də pəsawa so (oong seengglə)
a double room.	**um quarto de casal.** oong kooahrtoo də kazahl
We'll go right away.	**Vamos imediatamente.** vamoosh eemədeeahtamehngtə
How do I get there?	**Como é que vou para lá?** kawmoo e kə vaw para lah

At Airports

Where is the check-in/ transfer desk?	**Onde é que se faz o check-in/as transferências de vôo** awngde e kə sə fash oo check-in/ash trangshfərehngseeash də vawoo
Can I take this in the cabin?	**Posso levar isto para a cabine?** posoo ləvahr eeshtoo para a kahbeenə
Do I have to pay excess?	**Tenho que pagar excesso?** tenyoo kə pagahr əshsesoo
You haven't given me a luggage claim tag.	'**Não me deu um talão para a mala.** nowng mə dehoo oong talowng para a mahla

I've missed my flight. Can you give me another flight?	**Perdi o avião. Pode arranjar-me outro vôo?** pərdee oo aviowng. podə arrangzhahr-mə awtroo vawoo
When is the next flight to ...?	**Quando é o próximo voo para ...?** kooangdoo e oo proseemoo vawoo para
Is there a bar on the other side of the customs barrier?	**Há um bar do outro lado da alfândega?** ah oong bahr doo awtroo lahdoo da ahlfangdəga
Where is the flight indicator?	**Onde é o quadro de chegadas e partidas?** awngde e oo kooahdroo də shəgahdash ee parteedash
Is there a duty-free shop?	**Há free-shop?** ah free-shop
Is there another way to go up/down other than by escalator?	**Há outra maneira de subir/descer sem ser pelas escadas rolantes?** ah awtra manayra də soobeer/dəshsehr sayng sehr pehlash əshkahdash roolangtəsh
Where can I get some flight insurance?	**Aonde é que posso fazer um seguro de viagem?** aawngde e kə posoo fazehr oong səgooroo də veeahzhayng
Is there a wheelchair available?	**Há uma cadeira de rodas?** ah ooma kadayra də rrodash

At Railway Stations

Where is the ticket office?	**Onde é a bilheteira?** awngde e a bəllyətayra
One first-class/ second-class return ticket to Oporto.	**Um bilhete de ida e volta de primeira/segunda classe para o Porto.** oong bəllyehtə de eeda ee volta də preemayra/segoongda klahsə para oo pawrtoo
How much is a child's fare?	**Quanto é que custa um bilhete para criança?** kooangtoo e kə kooshta oong bəllyehtə para kreeangsa

Can I reserve a seat/a couchette/a sleeping berth?

Posso reservar um lugar/uma cabine/uma cama?
posoo rrəzərvahr oong loogahr/ooma kabeenə/ooma kama

Is there a supplement to pay?

Há algum suplemento a pagar?
ah ahlgoong soopləmehngtoo a pagahr

Do I have to change?

Tenho que mudar?
tenyoo kə moodahr

Will there be a restaurant car/buffet car on the train?

Há um restaurante/bar no comboio?
ah oong rrəshtowrangtə/bahr noo kawngboyoo

Where is the platform for the train to Faro?

Onde é a plataforma do comboio para Faro?
awngde e a plataforma doo kawngboyoo para Fahroo

Does my friend need a platform ticket?

O meu amigo precisa de bilhete de gare?
oo mehoo ameegoo prəseeza də bəllyehtə də gahrə

At what time does the train leave?

A que horas sai o comboio?
a kə orash sy oo kawngboyoo

At a Port

Which is quay number six?

Qual é o cais número seis?
kooahl e oo kysh nooməroo saysh

Where is the car ferry terminal?

Onde é o terminal do ferryboat?
awngde e oo tərmeenahl doo ferryboat

At what time can I go on board?

A que horas é que posso embarcar?
a kə orash e kə posoo ehngbarkahr

Will there be an announcement when visitors must disembark?

Anunciam a hora do desembarque?
anoongseeang a ora doo dəsehngbahrkə

What time does the boat leave?

A que horas é que sai o barco?
a kə orash e kə sy oo bahrkoo

VOCABULARY

bench	o banco	oo bangkoo
bus driver	o conductor	oo kawngdootawr
clock	o relógio	oo relozheeoo
gate	a porta	a porta
guard	o guarda	oo gooahrda
left luggage office	o depósito de bagagem	oo dəpozeetoo də bagahzhayng
lockers	os cacifos	oosh kaseefoosh
porter	o porteiro	oo poortayroo
security officer	o oficial de segurança	oo ofəseeahl də səgoorangsa
station buffet	o bar da estação	oo bahr da əshtasowng
station master	o chefe da estação	oo shefə da əshtasowng
tannoy	o auto-falante	oo owtoo-falangtə
ticket collector	o cobrador	oo koobradawr
vending machine	a máquina	a mahkeena
waiting room	a sala de espera	a sahla də əshpera

En Route

General Expressions

At what time do we start/take off?	**A que horas é que saimos/descolamos?** a kə orash e kə saeemoosh/dəshkoolamoosh
Why is there a delay?	**Porque é que está atrasado?** poorkə e kə əshtah atrazahdoo
Have I got time to go to the toilet?	**Tenho tempo de ir à casa de banho?** tenyoo tehngpoo də eer ah kahza də banyoo
I have mislaid my ticket.	**Não encontro o meu bilhete.** nowng ehngkawngtroo oo mehoo bəllyehtə
Take my address and passport number.	**Fique com a minha morada [o meu endereço] e o número do meu passaporte.** feekə kawng a meenya moorahda [oo mehoo ehngdərehsoo] ee oo noomeroo doo mehoo pahsaportə
Is this seat reserved?	**Este lugar está reservado?** ehshtə loogahr əshtah rrəzərvahdoo

Travelling by Air

Are you the Chief Steward/Stewardess?	**O senhor é o Comissário de bordo/a hospedeira [a moça aérea]?** oo sənyawr e oo koomeesahreeoo də bordoo/a oshpədayra [a mawsa aereea]
Which button do I press to call you?	**Qual é o botão para o (a) chamar?** kooahl e oo bootowng para oo (a) shamahr
Can you help me to adjust my seat?	**Ajuda-me a ajustar a minha cadeira?** azhooda-mə a azhooshtahr a meenya kadayra
Shall I fasten my seat belt?	**Devo apertar o cinto de segurança?** dehvoo apərtahr oo seengtoo də səgoorangsa

I haven't got a sick bag.	**Nao tenho saco de enjôo.**	nowng tenyoo sahkoo də ehngzhawoo
How high are we flying?	**A que altitude é que estamos a voar?**	a kə ahlteetoodə e kə əshtamoosh a vooahr
What speed are we doing?	**A que velocidade é que vamos?**	a kə vəlooseedahde e kə vamoosh
What town is that down below?	**Que cidade é essa aí em baixo?**	kə seedahde e esa aee ayng byshoo
Is there a map of the route?	**Há um mapa da rota?**	ah oong mahpa da rrota
Are there any duty-free goods available?	**Vendem artigos tax-free?**	vehngdayng arteegoosh tax-free
Can I pay you in foreign currency/English money?	**Posso pagar em moeda estrangeira/em moeda inglesa?**	posoo pagahr ayng mooeda əshtrangzhayra/ayng mooeda eengglehza
The airvent is stuck.	**O ar condicionado não funciona.**	oo ahr kawngdeeseeoonahdoo nowng foongseeawna
May I change my seat?	**Posso mudar de lugar?**	posoo moodahr də loogahr

VOCABULARY

aircraft	**o avião**	oo aveeowng
air terminal	**o terminal aéreo**	oo tərmeenahl aereeoo
arrival gate	**as chegadas**	ash shəgahdash
ashtray	**o cinzeiro**	oo seengzayroo
flight deck	**a coxia**	a koosheea
fuselage	**a fuselagem**	a foozəlahzhayng
jet engine	**o reactor**	oo reeahtawr
light	**a luz**	a loosh
luggage shelf	**a bagageira**	a bagazhayra
propeller	**a hélice**	a eleesə

tail	**a cauda**	a kowda
tray meal	**a refeição**	a rrəfaysowng
window	**a janela**	a zhanela
wing	**a asa**	a ahza

SIGNS

Aperte o cinto de segurança	Fasten your seat belt
Saída de emergência	Emergency exit
E proibido fumar	No smoking

Travelling by Rail

Is this the train for ...?
É este o comboio para ...?
e ehshtə oo kawngboeeoo para

Can you tell me where carriage 5 is?
Pode-me dizer onde é a carruagem número cinco?
podə-me dəzehr awngde e a karrooahzhayng noomeroo seengkoo

I have a couchette reservation.
Tenho uma cabine reservada.
tenyoo ooma kahbeenə rrəzərvahda

This is my seat reservation.
Este é o meu talão de reserva.
ehshtə e oo mehoo talowng də rrəserva

Is this seat taken?
Este lugar está ocupado?
ehshtə loogahr əshtah okoopahdoo

Is the dining car at the front or the back?
O restaurante é à frente ou atrás?
oo rrəshtowrangtə e ah frehngtə aw atrahsh

Two tickets for the first/ second service please.
Dois bilhetes para a primeira/ segunda rodada se faz favor.
doysh bəllyehtəsh para a preemayra/ səgoongda rroodahda se fahsh favawr

Is the buffet car open throughout the journey?
O bar está aberto durante toda a viagem?
oo bahr əshtah abertoo doorangtə tawda a veeahzhayng

Can I leave my big case in the baggage car?	**Posso deixar a minha mala grande na carruagem das malas?**	
	posoo dayshar a meenya mahla grangdə na karrooahzhayng dash mahlash	

Is there an observation car?	**Há uma carruagem panorâmica?**
	ah ooma karrooahzhayng panoorameeka

What station is this?	**Que estação é esta?**
	kə əshtasowng e eshta

The heating is on/off/ too high/too low.	**O aquecimento está ligado/desligado/muito alto/ muito baixo.**
	oo akeseemehngtoo əshtah leegahdoo/dəshleegahdoo/ mooeengtoo ahltoo/mooeengtoo byshoo

I can't open/close the window.	**Não consigo abrir/fechar a janela.**
	nowng kawngseegoo abreer/fəshahr a zhanela

Where do I have to change?	**Onde é que tenho que mudar?**
	awngde e kə tenyoo kə moodahr

Is this where I get my connection for ...?	**É aqui que tomo a ligação para ...?**
	e akee kə tomoo a leegasowng para

VOCABULARY

blanket	**o cobertor**	oo koobərtawr
corridor	**o corredor**	oo koorrədawr
compartment	**o compartimento**	oo kawngparteemehngtoo
cushion	**a almofada**	a ahlmoofahda
luggage rack	**a bagageira**	a bagazhayra
non smoking	**Não fumadores**	nowng foomadawrəsh
sleeping berth	**o beliche**	oo bəleeshə
sleeping car	**a carruagem cama**	a karrooahzhayng kama
sliding door	**a porta de correr**	a porta də koorrehr

Signs

Não se debruce da janela

Do not lean out of the window

Não utilize a casa de banho enquanto o comboio estiver na estaçâo

Do not use the toilet while the train is standing in the station

Travelling on a Steamer

Where is the purser's office?

Onde é o escritório do oficial de bordo?
awngde e oo əshkreetoreeoo doo ofəseeahl də bordoo

Can you show me my cabin?

Pode-me indicar qual é a minha cabine?
podə-mə eengdeekahr kooahl e a meenya kahbeenə

Are you the steward?

O senhor é o comissário?
o sənyawr e oo koomeesahreeoo

Is there a children's nursery/a shop/a gymnasium?

Há um infantário/uma loja/um ginásio?
ah oong eengfangtahreeoo/ooma lozha/oong zheenahzeeoo

Where can I get some seasick tablets?

Aonde é que posso arranjar comprimidos para o enjôo?
aawngde e kə posoo arrangzhar kawngprəmeedoosh para oo ehngzhawoo

On which side do we disembark?

De que lado é que desembarcamos?
də kə lahdoo e kə dəzehngbarkamoosh

The sea is calm/rough.

O mar está calmo/bravo.
oo mahr əshtah kahlmoo/ brahvoo

What are those birds? Seagulls?

O que é que são aqueles pássaros? Gaivotas?
oo kə e kə sowng akehləsh pahsaroosh? gyvotash

Is there a duty-free shop?

Há free-shop?
ah free-shop

VOCABULARY

aft	à popa	ah pawpa
anchor	a ancora	a angkoora
bridge	a ponte	a pawngtə
captain	o comandante	oo koomangdangtə
crew	a tripulação	a treepoolasowng
danger – propellers	atenção – hélices	atehngsowng – eleesəsh
deck	o deque	o dekə
funnel	a chaminé	a shameene
lifebelt	o colete de salvação	oo koolehtə də salvasowng
mast	o mastro	oo mahshtroo
officer	o oficial	oo ofəseeahl
port (harbour)	o porto	oo pawrtoo
port (left)	bombordo	bawngbordoo
radar	o radar	oo rrahdahr
raft	a jangada	a zhanggahda
rail	o gradeamento	oo gradeeamehngtoo
starboard	estibordo	əshteebordoo

Travelling by Coach

Is this the coach for Cintra?	**Esta é a camioneta para Sintra?** eshta e a kameeoneta para seengtra
Can I sit near the driver?	**Posso-me sentar perto do conductor?** posoo-mə sehngtahr pertoo doo kawngdootawr
Are the seats numbered?	**Os lugares estão numerados?** oosh loogahrəsh əstowng noomərahdoosh
Do I pay on the coach?	**Pago dentro da camioneta?** pahgoo dehngtroo da kameeoneta
Is there a stop en route?	**Paramos no caminho?** paramoosh noo kameenyo

Would you mind closing the window? It's draughty.	**Importa-se de fechar a janela? Há uma corrente de ar.**	
	eengporta-sə də fəshahr a zhanela? ah ooma koorrehngtə də ahr	
Can you help me with my luggage?	**Pode-me ajudar com a bagagem?**	
	podə-mə azhoodahr kawng a bagahzhayng	

VOCABULARY

back seat	**o banco de trás**	oo bangkoo də trahsh
driver	**o conductor**	oo kawngdootawr
foot rest	**o descanso**	oo dəshkangsoo
front seat	**o banco da frente**	oo bangkoo da frehngtə
guide	**o guia**	oo geea
luggage compartment	**o compartimento de bagagens**	oo kawngparteemehngtoo də bagahzhayngsh

Bus

Where is the bus stop?	**Onde é a paragem do autocarro?**	
	awngde e a parahzhayng doo owtokahrroo	
Does one have to queue?	**Tem que se fazer bicha [fila]?**	
	tayng kə sə fazehr beesha [feela]	
Can I buy a book of tickets?	**Posso comprar uma caderneta de bilhetes?**	
	posoo kawngprahr ooma kadərnehta də bəllyehtəsh	
Do you go by the Rossio?	**Quer ir pelo Rossio?**	
	ker eer pehloo rrooseeoo	
Will you tell me when we reach...?	**Pode-me chamar quando chegarmos a...?**	
	podə-mə shamahr kooangdoo shəgahrmoosh a	
I want to get off at the next stop.	**Quero sair na próxima paragem.**	
	kero saeer na proseema parahzhayng	
Will you ring the bell please?	**Pode tocar a campainha por favor?**	
	podə tookahr a kangpynya poor favawr	

I want to go to the Alfama.	**Quero ir a Alfama.** keroo eer a ahlfama
When is the first/ next/ last bus?	**Quando é o primeiro/ próximo/ último autocarro [ônibus]?** kooangdoo e oo preemayroo/ proseemoo/ oolteemoo owtokahrroo/ [awneeboos]

S<small>IGNS</small>

Paragem de autocarros [Parada de ônibus]	Bus stop
Reservado para deficientes motores	Reserved for disabled persons

Other Vehicles

Where can I hire a bicycle/a moped/a tricycle/a tandem?	**Onde é que posso alugar uma bicicleta/uma motorizada/um triciclo/um tandem?** awngde e kə posoo aloogahr ooma beeseekleta/ooma mootooreezahda/oong treeseekloo/oong tangdəm
Please put some air in this tyre.	**Se faz favor encha-me este pneu.** sə fahsh favawr ehngsha-mə ehshtə pnehoo
One of the spokes is broken.	**Um dos aros está partido.** oong doosh ahroosh əshtah parteedoo
The brake is not working.	**O travão não funciona.** oo travowng nowng foongseeawna
Do you have a bicycle with gears?	**Tem uma bicicleta com mudanças?** tehng ooma beeseekleta kawng moodangsash
The saddle is too high/ too low.	**O selim é alto demais/baixo demais.** oo səleeng e ahltoo dəmysh/byshoo dəmysh
Are there any horse-drawn vehicles at this resort?	**Há carruagens de cavalo nesta estação de férias?** ah karrooahzhayngsh də kavahloo neshta əshtasowng də fereeash
Will you put the roof down please?	**Pode fechar o tejadilho por favor?** podə fəshahr oo təzhadeellyoo poor favawr

Will you take the children in front?	**Pode levar as crianças à frente?** podə ləvahr ash kreeangsash ah frehngtə

VOCABULARY

bicycle pump	**a bomba de bicicleta**	a bawngba də beeseekleta
carrier	**o cesto**	oo sehshtoo
chain	**a corrente**	a koorrehngtə
crossbar	**a barra**	a bahrra
donkey	**o burro**	oo boorroo
handlebars	**o guiador**	oo geeadawr
harness	**o arreio**	oo arrayoo
lamp	**a lâmpada**	a langpada
mudguard	**o guarda lama**	oo gooahrda lama
pedal	**o pedal**	oo pədahl
rear light	**a luz traseira**	a loosh trazayra

Walking About

IN TOWN

Where is the main shopping street?	**Aonde é que são as lojas principais?** aawngde e kə sowng ash lozhash preengseepysh
Where is the town hall/police station?	**Onde é que é a Câmara Municipal [Perfeitura]/a esquadra [delegacia]** awngde e kə e a kamara moonəseepahl [perfaytoora]/a əshkooahdra [dələgaseea]
Can you direct me to the Tourist Office?	**Pode-me indicar onde é o Centro de Turismo?** podə-mə eengdeekahr awngde e oo sehngtroo də tooreeshmoo
In what part of the town are the theatres/ nightclubs?	**Aonde são os teatros nesta cidade/as boîtes nesta cidade?** aawngde sowng oosh teeahtroosh neshta seedahdə/ash booahtəsh neshta seedahdə

Can I get there by bus/ on foot?	**Posso ir de autocarro/a pé?**	posoo eer də owtokahrroo/a pe
Where is the nearest station/nearest bus stop/nearest taxi rank?	**Onde é a estação mais próxima/a paragem mais próxima/a praça de taxis mais próxima?**	awngdə e a əshtasowng mysh proseema/a parahzhayng mysh proseema/a prahsa də tahkseesh mysh proseema
Is there a market in the town?	**Há um mercado (uma praça) na cidade?**	ah oong mərkahdoo (ooma prahsa) na seedahdə
What day is market day?	**Qual é o dia de mercado?**	kooahl e oo deea də mərkahdoo
Is the business centre near?	**O centro comercial é perto?**	oo sehngtroo koomərseeahl e pertoo
Must one cross at the traffic lights?	**Tem que se atravessar nos semáforos?**	tehng kə sə atravəsahr noosh səmahfooroosh
Do pedestrians have right of way here?	**Os peões têm prioridade aqui?**	oosh peeoyngsh tayehng preeooreedahdə akee
Is there a public toilet near?	**Há uma casa de banho pública aqui perto?**	ah ooma kahza də banyoo poobleeka akee pertoo

Vocabulary

castle	**o castelo**	oo kashteloo
cathedral	**a catedral**	a katədrahl
cemetery	**o cemitério**	oo səmeetereeoo
church	**a igreja**	a eegrehzha
city centre	**o centro da cidade**	oo sehngtroo da seedahdə
concert hall	**a sala de concertos**	a sahla də kawngsehrtoosh
convent	**o convento**	oo kawngvehngtoo
courts	**os cortes**	oosh kortəsh
docks	**as docas**	ash dokash
exhibition	**a exposição**	a əshpoozeesowng
factory	**a fábrica**	a fahbreeka
fortress	**a fortaleza**	a foortalehza

fountain	**a fonte**	a fawngtə
gardens	**os jardins**	oosh zhardeengsh
Government buildings	**os edifícios de Estado**	oosh eedəfeeseeoosh də əshtahdoo
harbour	**o porto**	oo pawrtoo
lake	**o lago**	oo lahgoo
monastery	**o mosteiro**	oo mooshtayroo
monument	**o monumento**	oo moonoomehngtoo
museum	**o museu**	oo moozehoo
old town	**a cidade antiga**	a seedahdə angteega
opera house	**a ópera**	a opəra
palace	**o palácio**	oo palahseeoo
park	**o parque**	oo pahrkə
ruins	**as ruinas**	ash rrooeenash
shopping centre	**o centro comercial**	oo sehngtroo koomərseeahl
stadium	**o estádio**	oo əshtahdeeoo
statue	**a estátua**	a əshtahtooa
stock exchange	**a bolsa**	a bawlsa
subway	**o metro**	oo metroo
traffic lights	**os semáforos**	oosh səmahfooroosh
tower	**a torre**	a tawrrə
university	**a universidade**	a ooneɛvərseedahdə
zoo	**o jardim zoológico**	oo zhardeeng zoolozheekoo

In The Country

May we walk through here?	**Podemos ir por aqui?** poodehmoosh eer poor akee
Is this a public footpath?	**Este é um caminho público?** eshtə e oong kameenyoo poobleekoo
Do I need permission to fish?	**Preciso de licença para pescar?** prəseezoo də leesehngsa para pəshkahr
Which way is north/south/west/east?	**Onde fica o norte/sul/este/oeste?** awngdə feeka oo nortə/sool/eshtə/oeshtə

Is there a bridge or ford across this stream?	**Há uma ponte ou um vau que atravessa este riacho?**	
	ah ooma **pawngt**ə aw oong vow kə atravesa **ehsht**ə reeahshoo	
How far is the nearest village?	**A que distância fica a aldeia mais próxima?**	
	a kə dəstangseea feeka a ahldaya mysh **pro**seema	
I am lost. Can you please direct me to...?	**Perdi-me. Pode-me mostrar o caminho para...?**	
	pərdee-mə. podə-mə mooshtrahr oo kameenyoo para	
Will you please show me the route on this map?	**Pode-me mostrar o caminho neste mapa se faz favor?**	
	podə-mə mooshtrahr oo kameenyoo nehshtə mahpa sə fash favawr	

VOCABULARY

bird	**o pássaro**	oo pahsaroo
brook	**o riacho**	oo reeahshoo
cat	**o gato**	oo gahtoo
cliff	**a falésia**	a falezeea
cottage	**a casa pequena**	a kahza pəkehna
cow	**a vaca**	a vahka
dog	**o cão**	oo kowng
farm	**a quinta [a fazenda]**	a keengta [a fazehngda]
field	**o campo**	oo kangpoo
footpath	**o caminho**	oo kameenyoo
forest	**a floresta**	a flooreshta
goat	**a cabra**	a kahbra
heath	**a charneca**	a sharneka
hill	**o monte**	oo mawngtə
horse	**o cavalo**	oo kavahloo
inn	**a estalagem**	a əshtalahzhayng
lake	**o lago**	oo lahgoo
marsh	**terra pantanosa**	terra pangtanoza
moorland	**o descampado**	oo dəshkangpahdoo
mountain	**a montanha**	a mawngtanya
orchard	**o pomar**	oo poomahr

peak	o cimo	oo seemoo
pig	o porco	oo pawrkoo
pond	o lago	oo lahgoo
river	o rio	oo rreeoo
sea	o mar	oo mahr
sheep	os carneiros	oosh karnayroosh
spring	a fonte	a fawngtə
stream	o ribeiro	oo reebayroo
swamp	o pântano	oo pangtanoo
tree	a árvore	a ahrvoorə
valley	o vale	oo vahlə
village	a aldeia	a ahldaya
vineyard	a vinha	a veenya
waterfall	a queda de água	a keda də ahgooa
wood	o bosque	oo boshkə

Motoring

At the Frontier

Here is	Está aqui
	əshtah akee
my registration book.	a minha caderneta.
	a meenya kadərnehta
my green card insurance.	o meu seguro internacional.
	oo mehoo səgooroo eengtərnaseeoonahl
my driving licence.	a minha carta de condução.
	a meenya kahrta də kawngdoosowng

I have an international licence.	Tenho carta internacional.
	tenyoo kahrta eengtərnaseeoonahl

This is a translation of my British licence.	Isto é uma tradução da minha carta inglesa.
	eeshtoo e ooma tradoosowng da meenya kahrta eengglehza

This is a hired car.	Este carro é alugado.
	eshtə kahrroo e aloogahdoo

Here are the documents.	**Estão aqui os documentos.** əshtowng akee oosh dookoomehngtoosh
Do you want to open the boot?	**Quer abrir a mala?** ker abreer a mahla
I arrived today.	**Cheguei hoje.** shəgay awzhə
I am staying for two weeks.	**Fico cá duas semanas.** feekoo kah dooash səmanash
We are passing through on the way to Spain.	**Estamos de passagem para Espanha.** əshtamoosh də pasahzhayng para əshpanya
Does this customs post close at night?	**Este centro alfandegário fecha à noite?** ehshtə sehngtroo ahlfangdəgahreeoo faysha ah noytə.
Do you want me to stop the engine?	**Quer que eu desligue o motor?** ker kə ehoo dəshleegə oo mootawr

On the Road

Portugal is on the whole a mountainous country with the only flat region to the south of Lisbon in the Alentejo. The roads are often winding and of indifferent quality except for the main roads which run along the coast or inland towards Spanish frontier posts. There are only two short sections of motorway, from Lisbon and from Oporto. Driving is on the right and at crossroads and roundabouts precedence is given to traffic entering from the *right* unless otherwise indicated.

Can you tell me how to get to Óbidos?	**Pode-me indicar o caminho para Óbidos?** podə-mə eendeekahr oo kameenyoo para obeedoosh
How many kilometres is it?	**Quantos quilómetros são?** kooangtoosh keeloomətroosh sowng
Is it a good road?	**A estrada é boa?** a əshtrahda e bawa

Is it hilly or flat?	**É montanhosa ou plana?** e mawngtanyoza aw plana
Is it straight or winding?	**É recta ou tem muitas curvas?** e reta aw tayng mooeengtash koorvash
What is the speed limit on this section?	**Qual é o limite de velocidade aqui?** kooahl e oo leemeetə də vəlooseedahdə akee
Will you point out the route on this map, please?	**Pode-me indicar o caminho neste mapa, se faz favor?** podə-mə eengdeekahr oo kameenyoo nehshtə mahpa sə fahsh favawr
I am sorry I have no change.	**Desculpe, não tenho troco.** dəshkoolpə nowng tenyoo trawkoo
How far is it to the next petrol station?	**Qual é a distância até à próxima estação de gasolina?** kooahl e a dəshtangseea ate ah proseema əshtasowng də gazooleena
I want twenty-five litres, please.	**Quero vinte cinco litros, por favor.** keroo veengtə seengkoo leetroosh poor favawr
Give me 500 escudos' worth.	**Meta quinhentos escudos.** mehta keenyehngtoosh əshkoodoosh
Fill her up, please.	**Encha o depósito, se faz favor.** ehngsha oo dəpozeetoo sə fahsh favawr
Please check the oil and water.	**Se faz favor verifique o óleo e a água.** sə fahsh favawr vəreefeekə oo oleeoo ee a ahgooa
I need some air in the tyres.	**Preciso de meter ar nos pneus.** prəseezoo də mətehr ahr noosh pnehoosh
I think the windscreen wiper fluid needs topping up.	**Acho que preciso de mais líquido para os limpa pára-brisas.** ahshoo kə prəseezoo də mysh leekeedoo para oosh leengpa pahra breezash
Have you any distilled water for the battery?	**Tem água destilada para a bateria?** tehng ahgooa dəshteelahda para a batəreea

Please clean the windscreen.	**Pode limpar o pára-brisas se faz favor.**
	podə leengpahr oo pahra breezas sə fahsh favawr
Have you any paper towels?	**Tem toalhas de papel?**
	tehng tooahllyash də papel
Have you got a carwash?	**Tem lavagem automática?**
	tehng lavahzhayng owtoomahteeka
Do you sell yellow filters for the headlights?	**Vendem filtros amarelos para os faróis?**
	vehngdayng feeltroosh amareloosh para oosh faroeesh
Can I park here?	**Posso estacionar aqui?**
	posoo əshtaseeoonahr akee
Where is the nearest car park?	**Onde é o parque de estacionamento mais próximo?**
	awngde e oo pahrkə də əshtaseeoonamehngtoo mysh proseemoo.

Trouble with the Police

Usually the police are polite and helpful to visitors, but they are more likely to be so if you appear friendly and co-operative. A few phrases in their language can sometimes work miracles.

I'm sorry. I did not see your signal.	**Desculpe. Não vi o seu sinal.**
	dəshkoolpə nowng vee oo sehoo seenahl
I thought I had right of way.	**Julgava que tinha prioridade.**
	zhoolgahva kə teenya preeooreedahdə
I apologize. I won't do it again.	**Peço desculpa. Não volto a fazer.**
	pesoo dəshkoolpa. nowng voltoo a fazehr

Here is my name and address.	**Está aqui o meu nome e a minha morada [o meu endereço]** əshtah akee oo mehoo nawmə ee a meenya moorahda [oo mehoo ehngdərehsoo]
This is my passport.	**Este é o meu passaporte.** ehshtə e oo mehoo pahsaportə
Do I have to pay a fine?	**Tenho que pagar uma multa?** tenyoo kə pagahr ooma moolta
How much?	**Quanto?** kooangtoo
I haven't got any cash on me. Can I settle up at a police station?	**Não trago dinheiro comigo. Posso pagar numa esquadra [delegacia]?** nowng trahgoo dənyayroo koomeegoo posoo pagahr nooma əshkooahdra [dələgaseea]
Thank you for your courtesy.	**Obrigado(a) pela atenção.** obreegahdoo(a) pehla atehngsowng

Car Rental

I want to hire	**Quero alugar** keroo aloogahr
a small car	**um carro pequeno.** oong kahrroo pəkehnoo
a family saloon.	**um carro de turismo.** oong kahrroo de tooreezhmoo
a large car.	**um carro grande.** oong kahrroo grangdə
a sports car.	**um carro de desporto.** oong kahrroo de dəshpawrtoo
a van.	**uma carrinha.** ooma karreenya
I shall need it for ...days.	**Vou precisar dele durante ...dias.** vaw prəseezahr dehlə doorangtə ...deeash

How much is the daily charge?	**Quanto é que custa por dia?** kooangtoo e kə kooshta poor deea
Is it cheaper by the week?	**Sai mais barato o aluguer à semana?** sy mysh barahtoo oo alooger ah səmana
Does that include mileage and third party insurance?	**Inclui quilometragem e seguro contra terceiros?** eengklooee keeloomətrahzhayng ee səgooroo kawngtra tersayroosh
Is the insurance fully comprehensive?	**O seguro é contra todos os riscos?** oo səgooroo e kawngtra tawdoosh oosh rreeshkoosh
What is the mileage charge?	**Qual é o preço por quilómetro?** kooahl e oo prehsoo poor keelomətroo
Where do I pick up the car?	**Aonde é que vou buscar o carro?** aawngde e kə vaw booshkahr oo kahrroo
Can you bring it to my hotel?	**Pode trazê-lo ao meu hotel?** podə trazeh-loo ow mehoo otel
Can I leave it at another town or at the airport?	**Posso deixá-lo noutra cidade ou no aeroporto?** posoo dayshah-loo nawtra seedahdə aw noo aeropawrtoo
Is there a deposit to pay?	**Há algum depósito a pagar?** ah ahlgoong dəpozeetoo a pagahr
May I pay with my credit card?	**Posso pagar com o meu cartão de crédito?** posoo pagahr kawng oo mehoo kartowng də kredeetoo
Will you please check the documents with me?	**Pode-me ajudar a verificar os documentos?** podə-mə azhoodahr a vəreefeekahr oosh dookoomehngtoosh
Will you show me the gears and instrument panel?	**Pode-me mostrar as mudanças e o painel de instrumentos?** podə-mə mooshtrahr ash moodangsash ee oo pynel də eengstroomehngtoosh
Is the tank full?	**O depósito está cheio?** oo dəpozeetoo əshtah shayoo

Road Signs

Alfândega	Customs
Alto	Halt/Stop
Acender as luzes	Lights on
Atencão	Caution
Auto-estrada	Motorway
Bifurcação	Road forks
Cruzamento perigoso	Dangerous crossing
Curva perigosa	Dangerous bend
Dê passagem	Give way
Descida perigosa	Steep hill
Desvio	Diversion
Devagar	Slow
Entrada	Entry
Escola	School
Espere/Pare	Wait/Halt
Estacionamento permitido	Parking allowed
Estacionamento proibido	No parking
Estrada estreita	Road narrows
Estrada fechada	Road closed
Gelo	Ice
Guiar com cuidado	Drive with care
Lentamente	Slowly
Obras	Road works
Parar/Pare	Stop
Parque de estacionamento	Car park
Passagem de gado	Cattle crossing
Passagem de nível	Level crossing
Peões	Pedestrians
Perigo!	Danger!
Polícia	Police
Ponte estreita	Narrow bridge
Portagem	Toll
Proibida a entrada	No entry
Proibido ultrapassar	No overtaking
Prudência	Caution
Queda de pedras	Falling rocks

Reduza a velocidade	Reduce speed
Rua sem saída	Cul de sac
Saída	Exit
Saída de camiões	Exit for lorries
Sentido proibido	No entry
Sentido único	One way
Veículos pesados	(For) heavy vehicles
Velocidade máxima	Maximum speed

Trouble on the Road

OTHER PEOPLE'S

There has been an accident on the road five kilometres back.
Houve um desastre na estrada cinco quilómetros atrás.
awvə oong dəzahshtrə na əshtrahda seengkoo keelomətroosh atrahsh

Will you phone the police, please?
Pode telefonar para a polícia, por favor?
podə tələfoonahr para a pooleeseea poor favawr

No, I did not see it happen.
Não, não vi o que aconteceu.
nowng, nowng vee oo kə akawngtəsehoo

The car registration number was...
A matrícula do carro era...
a matreekoola doo kahrroo era

I do not think anyone is hurt.
Parece-me que ninguém está ferido.
paresə-mə kə neenggayng əshtah fəreedoo

Someone is badly hurt.
Há uma pessoa gravemente ferida.
ah ooma pəsawa grahvəmehngtə fəreeda

YOURS

Are you all right?
Está bem?
əshtah bayng

My passengers are not hurt.
Os meus passageiros não estão feridos.
oosh mehoosh pasazhayroosh nowng əshtowng fəreedoosh

The car is damaged.	**O carro está amachucado.** oo **kah**rroo əsh**tah** amashoo**kah**doo
May I have your insurance details?	**Pode-me dar os detalhes do seu seguro?** **pod**ə-mə dahr oosh də**tahll**yəsh doo **seh**oo sə**goo**roo
Your name and address, please?	**O seu nome e morada, por favor?** oo **seh**oo **nawm**ə ee moo**rahd**a poor fa**vawr**
Will you please fill out this form?	**Pode preencher este formulário, por favor?** **pod**ə pree-**ehng**shehr **ehsht**ə foormoo**lah**reeoo poor fa**vawr**
I think we shall have to call the police.	**Parece-me que temos que chamar a polícia.** pa**res**ə-mə kə **teh**moosh kə sha**mahr** a poo**lee**seea
Excuse me, would you mind being a witness?	**Desculpe, importa-se de ser testemunha?** dəsh**koolp**ə, eeng**port**a-sə də sehr təsh**tə**moonya
It happened because he put his brakes on suddenly.	**Aconteceu porque ele travou de repente.** akawngtə**seh**oo **poork**ə **ehl**ə tra**vaw** də rrə**pehngt**ə
He came out of a side road without signalling.	**Ele saiu de uma transversal sem fazer sinal.** **ehl**ə sa**eeoo** də **oom**a trangzh**vər**sahl sayng fa**zehr** see**nahl**
He tried to overtake on a narrow stretch of road.	**Ele tentou ultrapassar numa parte de estrada estreita.** **ehl**ə tehng**taw** ooltrapa**sahr** **noom**a **pahrt**ə də əsh**trahd**a əsh**trayt**a
He turned off without signalling.	**Ele virou sem fazer sinal.** **ehl**ə vee**raw** sayng fa**zehr** see**nahl**
May I explain to someone who understands English?	**Posso explicar a alguém que perceba inglês?** **pos**oo əshplee**kahr** a ahl**gayng** kə pər**sehb**a eeng**glehsh**

If you are unfortunate enough to have an accident, be sure to get all the details from the other driver involved. Your insurance company will have provided you with an accident report form. Fill it up on the spot with the help of the other driver. Above all, keep cool.

Breakdown

If you have a breakdown put out the red triangle behind the car at once or you may be penalized. Get your car off the road if possible.

Thank you for stopping. I am in trouble. Will you help me?	**Obrigado por ter parado. Estou com um problema. Pode ajudar-me?** obreegahdoo poor tehr parahdoo. eshtaw kawng oong prooblehma. podə azhoodahr-mə
My car has broken down.	**O meu carro avariou-se.** oo mehoo kahrroo avareeaw-sə
I have locked myself out of the car.	**Tranquei o carro com as chaves lá dentro.** trangkay oo kahrroo kawng ash shahvəsh lah dehngtroo
Will you tell the next garage or breakdown service vehicle if you see one?	**Pode avisar a próxima garagem ou o próximo reboque, se vir algum?** podə aveezahr a proseema garahzhayng aw oo proseemoo rrəbokə sə veer ahlgoong
Will you please telephone a garage for me?	**Pode-me telefonar para a garagem?** podə-mə tələfoonahr para a garahzhayng
Can you give me a lift to the next telephone?	**Pode dar-me uma boleia até ao próximo telefone?** podə dahr-mə ooma boolaya ate ow proseemoo tələfonə
Can you send a breakdown truck?	**Pode mandar um reboque?** podə mangdahr oong rrəbokə
I am five kilometres from the last entry.	**Estou a cinco quilómetros da última entrada.** əshtaw a seengkoo keelomətroosh da oolteema ehngtrahda
I am three kilometres from Lisbon on the motorway.	**Estou a três quilómetros de Lisboa na auto-estrada.** əshtaw a seengkoo keelomətroosh də leeshbawa na owtoo-eshtrahda

How long will you be?	**Quanto tempo vai demorar?** kooangtoo tehngpoo vy dəmoorahr

Repairs

There's something wrong with the engine.	**O motor não funciona bem.** oo mootawr nowng foongseeawna bayng
The clutch is slipping.	**A embraiagam está a patinar.** a ehngbryahzhayng əstah a pateenahr
There is a noise from the...	**Há um barulho no...** ah oong baroollyoo noo
The brakes are not working.	**Os travões não funcionam.** oosh travoyngsh nowng foongseeawnang
The cooling system is leaking.	**O sistema de arrefecimento tem uma fuga.** oo səstehma də arrəfeseemehngtoo tayng ooma fooga
My fan belt is broken.	**A minha correia de ventoinha está partida.** a meenya koorraya də vehngtooeenya əshtah parteeda
I've got a flat tyre.	**Tenho um pneu furado.** tenyoo oong pnehoo foorahdoo
Would you please mend this puncture?	**Pode remendar este furo?** podə rrəmehngdahr ehshtə fooroo
The electrical system isn't working.	**O sistema eléctrico não funciona.** oo səshtehma eeletreekoo nowng foongseeawna
The engine is overheating.	**O motor está a aquecer demais.** oo mootawr əshtah a akesehr dəmysh
The car won't start.	**O carro não pega.** oo kahrroo nowng pega
What is the matter?	**O que é que se passa?** oo kə e ka sə pahsa

Is it	**Está**
	əshtah
broken?	**avariado?**
	avareeahdoo
burnt out?	**queimado?**
	kaymahdoo
disconnected?	**desligado?**
	dəshleegahdoo
jammed?	**encravado?**
	ehngkravahdoo
leaking?	**a pingar?**
	a peengahr

Has it short-circuited?	**Houve um curto-circuito?**
	awvə oong **koo**rtoo-seer**koo**eetoo

Do I need a new part?	**É preciso uma peça nova?**
	e prəseezoo ooma pesa nova

Is there a Ford agent in town?	**Há um representante da Ford na cidade?**
	ah oong rəprəzehng**tang**tə da ford na see**dah**də

Can you send for the part?	**Pode encomendar a peça?**
	podə ehngkoomehng**dah**r a pesa

Is it serious?	**É sério?**
	e sereeoo

How long will it take to repair?	**Quanto tempo leva a arranjar?**
	kooangtoo **teh**ngpoo leva a arrang**zhah**r

Can I hire another car?	**Posso alugar outro carro?**
	posoo aloo**gah**r awtroo **kah**rroo

What will it cost?	**Quanto é que vai custar?**
	kooangtoo e kə vy koo**shtah**r

I will get the part flown from Britain.	**Mando vir a peça de Inglaterra de avião.**
	mangdoo veer a pesa də eeng**glah**terra də aveeowng

Your mechanic has been very kind. I would like to tip him.	**O seu mecânico foi muito simpático. Queria dar-lhe uma gorgeta.** oo sehoo məkanæekoo foy mooeengtoo seengpahteekoo. kəreea dahr-llyə ooma goorzhehta

VOCABULARY

battery	**a bateria**	a batəreea
bearings	**os rulamentos**	oosh roolamehngtoosh
brake lining	**o calço dos travões**	oo kahlsoo doosh travoyngsh
brakes	**os travões**	oosh travoyngsh
bulbs	**as lâmpadas**	ash langpadash
carburettor	**o carburador**	oo karbooradawr
clutch	**a embraiagem**	a ehngbryahzhayng
cooling system	**o sistema de arrefecimento**	oo səshtehma de arrəfeseemehngtoo
dip switch	**o contrôlo de luzes**	oo kawngtrawloo də loozəsh
distributor	**o distribuidor**	oo dəshtreebooeedawr
dynamo	**o dínamo**	oo deenamoo
electrical system	**o sistema eléctrico**	oo səshtehma eeletreekoo
exhaust pipe	**o tubo de escape**	oo tooboo də əshkahpə
fan	**a ventoinha**	a vehngtooeenya
filter	**o filtro**	oo feeltroo
fuel pump	**a bomba de gasolina**	a bawngba de gazooleena
fuel tank	**o depósito de gasolina**	oo dəpozeetoo də gazooleena
gears	**as mudanças**	ash moodangsash
generator	**o gerador**	oo zheradawr
hand brake	**o travão de mão**	oo travowng də mowng
headlights	**os faróis**	oosh faroeesh
heating system	**a aquecimento**	oo akeseemehngtoo
horn	**a buzina**	a boozeena
ignition	**a ignição**	a eegneesowng
indicator	**o pisca-pisca**	oo peeshka-peeshka

lubrication system	o sistema de lubrificação	oo səshtehma de loobreefeekasowng
points	os platinados	oosh plateenahdoosh
radiator	o radiador	oo rrahdeeadawr
reflector	o reflector	oo rrəfletawr
seat	o assento	oo asehngtoo
sidelights	os mínimos	oosh meeneemoosh
silencer	o silenciador	oo seelehngseeadawr
sparking plug	a vela	a vela
starter motor	o motor de arranque	oo mootawr de arrangkə
suspension	a suspensão	a sooshpehngsowng
transmission	a transmissão	a trangshmeesowng
wheels	as rodas	ash rrodash
windscreen	o para-brisas	oo pahra breezash
windscreen wipers	os limpa pára-brisas	oosh leengpa pahra breezash

A Place to Stay

There are places to suit every budget level in Portugal, from great four-
and five-star hotels at the seaside resorts to simple inns with rooms to let. If
you have not already booked your hotel room when you arrive ask the
local branch of the Portuguese Tourist Office for help.

In Portugal there are government-owned hotels and inns called **pousadas**
which are often in buildings of historical interest. Inns are known as
estalagens and a boarding house is a **pensão.** If you are a do-it-yourself fan
you will find plenty of apartments and villas to let and camping sites are
free.

Hotels are classified by a three, two or one-star system.

Pousada   Government establishment. Maximum stay five days.
Pensão   Boarding house.
Quarto   A room.

The hotels in the principal cities of Brazil range from deluxe to pensions.
Most of them quote on a room-only basis but meals are available. In the
country villages standards are lower and accommodation meagre.

Hotels and Pensions

Finding a Room

I am travelling with the ...travel agency.	**Estou a viajar [estou viajando] com a agência de viagens...** əshtaw a veeazhahr [əshtaw veeazhangdoo] kawng a azhehngseea de veeahzhayngsh
Here is my hotel coupon.	**Está aqui o meu cupão de hotel.** əshtah akee oo mehoo koopowng də otel
My room is already reserved.	**O meu quarto já está marcado.** oo mehoo kooahrtoo zhah əshtah markahdoo

I am travelling independently.	**Estou a viajar independentemente.** əshtaw a veeazhahr eengdəpehngdehngtəmehngtə
Will a porter bring my luggage in?	**O porteiro traz a minha bagagem para dentro?** oo poortayroo trahsh a meenya bagahzhayng para dehngtroo
Can I leave my car here?	**Posso deixar o carro aqui?** posoo dayshahr oo kahrroo akee
Is there a car park?	**Há um parque de estacionamento?** ah oong pahrkə də əshtaseeoonamehngtoo
Are you the receptionist/porter/manager?	**O senhor é o recepcionista/o porteiro/o gerente?** oo sənyawr e oo rreseseeooneeshta/oo poortayroo/oo zhərehngtə
Have you	**Tem** tehng
a single room?	**um single?** oong seengglə
a double room?	**um quarto duplo?** oong kooahrtoo dooploo
a three-bedded room?	**un quarto com três camas?** oong kooahrtoo kawng trehsh kamash
Have you a room	**Tem um quarto** tehng oong kooahrtoo
with twin beds?	**com duas camas?** kawng dooash kamash
with a full-size bath and separate toilet?	**com uma banheira grande e retrete separada?** kawng ooma banyayra grangdə ee rrətretə səparahda
with a bath or shower?	**com banheira ou duche?** kawng banyayra aw dooshə
with a balcony?	**com varanda?** kawng varangda
looking over the front/back?	**com vista para a frente/trás?** kawng veeshta para a frehngtə/trahsh
How much is it per day/per week?	**Quanto custa por dia/por semana?** kooangtoo kooshta poor deea/poor səmana

Do you do	**Tem sistema de**
	tehng səshtehma də
bed and breakfast/ demi pension?	**quarto e pequeno almoço/meia-pensão?**
	kooahrtoo ee pəkehnoo almawsoo/**may**a pehngsowng
Is there a reduction	**Há uma reducção**
	ah ooma rədoosowng
for a longer stay/for children?	**para uma estadia prolongada/para crianças?**
	para ooma əshtadeea proolawngahda/para kreeangsash
Are there special mealtimes for children?	**Há horas especiais para as refeições das crianças?**
	ah orash əshpeseeysh para ash rəfaysoyngsh dash kreeangsash
I don't want to pay more than... escudos per day.	**Não quero pagar mais do que... escudos por dia.**
	nowng keroo pagahr mysh doo kə... əshkoodoosh poor deea
Have you anything cheaper?	**Tem alguma coisa mais barata?**
	tehng ahl**goo**ma koyza mysh barahta
Do I have to fill in a visitor's card?	**Tenho que preencher um cartão de visita?**
	tenyoo kə pree-ehngshehr oong kartowng də vəzeeta
Here is my passport.	**Está aqui o meu passaporte.**
	əshtah akee oo mehoo pahsaportə
How long will you keep it?	**Quanto tempo é que o vai guardar?**
	kooangtoo tehngpoo e kə oo vy gooardahr
I'd like to go up to my room right away.	**Queria ir já para o meu quarto.**
	kəreea eér zhah para oo mehoo kooahrtoo
Will you send up the luggage?	**Pode mandar subir as malas?**
	podə mangdahr soobeer ash mahlash
This case is for room 3 and that one is for Number 12.	**Esta mala é para o quarto número três e essa é para o número doze.**
	eshta mahla e para oo kooahrtoo noomeroo trehsh ee esa e para oo noomeroo dawzə
May I have the room key?	**Dá-me a chave do quarto?**
	dah-mə a shahvə doo kooahrtoo

| Is the key in the door? | **A chave está na porta?** |
| | a shahvə əshtah na porta |

| Where is the lift? Do I work it myself? | **Onde é que é o elevador? Posso subir sózinho?** |
| | awngde e kə e oo eeləvadawr. posoo soobeer sozeenyoo |

| Can you put all the extras on my bill? | **Pode pôr todos os extras na minha conta?** |
| | podə pawr tawdoosh oosh ayshtrash na meenya kawngta |

| Is there a post box in the hotel? | **Há uma caixa postal no hotel?** |
| | ah ooma kysha pooshtahl noo otel |

| Can you get the daily papers for me? | **Pode-me arranjar os jornais diários?** |
| | podə-mə arrangzhahr oosh zhoornysh deeahreeoosh |

Moving In

This room is	**Este quarto é**
	eshtə kooahrtoo e
too small.	**pequeno demais.**
	pəkehnoo dəmysh
too large.	**grande demais.**
	grangdə dəmysh
too noisy.	**barulhento demais.**
	baroollyehngtoo dəmysh
too dark.	**escuro demais.**
	əshkooroo dəmysh
too high up.	**num andar alto demais.**
	noong angdahr ahltoo dəmysh

| Haven't you got a double bed? | **Não tem cama de casal?** |
| | nowng tehng kama də kazahl |

| Can you please make the twin beds into one double? | **Pode juntar as duas camas para fazer cama de casal?** |
| | podə zhoongtahr ash dooash kamash para fazehr ooma kama də kazahl |

| I shall need | **Vou precisar de** |
| | vaw prəseezahr də |

another pillow.	**outra almofada.**
	awtra ahlmoofahda
another blanket.	**outro cobertor.**
	awtroo koobərtawr
another clothes hanger.	**outro cabide.**
	awtroo kabeedə
a child's cot.	**um berço para criança.**
	oong behrsoo para kreeangsa

| The bedside light is not working. The bulb is broken. | **O candeeiro da mesinha de cabeceira não funciona. A lâmpada está fundida.** |
| | oo kangdeeayroo da məzeenya də kabəsayra nowng foongseeawna. a langpada əshtah foongdeeda |

| Which is the hot/cold tap? | **Qual é a torneira de água quente/fria?** |
| | kooahl e a toornayra də ahgooa kehngtə/freea |

| Is this the electric razor socket? | **Esta é ficha para a máquina de barbear?** |
| | eshta e a feesha para a mahkeena də barbeeahr |

| What is the voltage here? | **Qual é a corrente eléctrica aqui?** |
| | kooahl e a koorrehngtə eeletreeka akee |

| My plug won't fit. | **A minha tomada não cabe.** |
| | a meenya toomahda nowng kahbə |

| Have you got an adaptor? | **Tem um transformador?** |
| | tehng oong trangshfoormadawr |

| Is there an electrician in the village? | **Há um electricista na aldeia?** |
| | ah oong eeletrəseeshta na ahldaya |

| Is there a hotel laundry? | **Há uma lavandaria no hotel?** |
| | ah ooma lavangdareea noo otel |

| Are there facilities for washing and ironing? | **Tem lavandaria e quarto de engomar?** |
| | tehng lavangdareea ee kooahrtoo də ehngoomahr |

| The blind is stuck. | **A persiana está encravada.** |
| | a pərseeana əshtah ehngkravahda |

| Will you bring a bottle of drinking water? | **Pode trazer uma garrafa de água se faz favor?** |
| | podə trazehr ooma garrahfa də ahgooa se fahsh favawr |

Can I leave valuables in the hotel safe? **Posso deixar objectos de valor no cofre do hotel?** posoo dayshahr obzhetoosh də valawr noo kofrə doo otel

What time is breakfast/lunch/ dinner? **A que horas é o pequeno-almoço [o café da manhã]/o almoço/o jantar?** a kə orash e oo pəkehnoo ahlmawsoo [oo kafe da manyang]/oo ahlmawsoo/oo zhangtahr

Do you serve breakfast in bed? **Servem pequeno-almoço na cama?** servayng pəkehnoo ahlmawsoo na kama

Does the hotel do packed lunches? **O hotel prepara pique-niques?** oo otel prəpahra peekə-neekəsh

Small Hotels and Pensions

Do you have set times for meals? **Há horas marcadas para as refeições?** ah orash markahdash para ash rəfaysoyngsh

May I have a towel and soap? **Arranja-me uma toalha e sabonete?** arrangzha-mə ooma tooahllya ee saboonehtə

At what time do you lock the front door at night? **A que horas é que fecham a porta principal à noite?** a kə orash e kə fayshang a porta preengseepahl ah noytə

May I have a key? **Arranja-me uma chave?** arrangzha-mə ooma shahvə

Is it all right to leave the car in the street? **Posso deixar o carro na rua?** posoo dayshahr oo kahrroo na rrooa

Will our things be safe? **As nossas coisas ficam seguras?** ash nosash koyzash feekang səgoorash

Where is the nearest garage? **Qual é a garagem mais próxima?** kooahl e a gahrahzhayng mysh proseema

Rooms in Private Houses

Do you have a room free?	**Tem um quarto vago?** tehng oong kooahrtoo vahgoo
Do you do breakfast?	**Servem pequeno-almoço?** servayng pəkehnoo ahlmawsoo
Is there a café nearby?	**Há algum café aqui ao pé?** ah ahlgoong kafe akee ow pe
Would you like me to pay now?	**Quer que pague já?** ker kə pahgə zhah
At what time will it be convenient to use the bathroom?	**A que horas é que posso utilizar a casa de banho?** a kə orash e kə posoo ootəleezahr a kahza də banyoo
Do I need to tell you if I have a bath?	**É preciso dizer quando tomo banho?** e prəseezoo deezehr kooangdoo tomoo banyoo
Could you wake us in the morning?	**Pode acordar-nos de manhã?** podə akoordahr-noosh də manyang
Is there a lounge?	**Há uma sala de estar?** ah ooma sahla də əshtahr
Shall I lock my room?	**Fecho a porta do quarto à chave?** fayshoo a porta doo kooahrtoo ah shahvə

Paying the Bill

May I have my bill, please?	**Dá-me a conta se faz favor?** dah-mə a kawngta sə fahsh favawr
Will you prepare my bill for first thing tomorrow?	**Pode ter a minha conta pronta amanhã cedo?** podə tehr a meenya kawngta prawngta ahmanyang sehdoo
I think there is a mistake.	**Acho que há um engano.** ahshoo kə ah oong ehngganoo

I don't understand this item.	**Não percebo esta parcela.**	
	nowng persehboo eshta parsela	
May I pay by cheque? I have a Eurocheque card.	**Posso pagar com cheque? Tenho um cartão Eurocheque.**	
	posoo pagahr kawng shekə? tenyoo oong kartowng ehooroshekə	
Do you accept credit cards?	**Aceitam cartões de crédito?**	
	asaytang kartoyngsh də kredeetoo	
Is service included?	**O serviço está incluido?**	
	oo sərveesoo əshtah eengklooeedoo	
Is VAT included?	**A taxa está incluida?**	
	a tahsha əshtah eengklooeeda	
May I have a receipt please?	**Dá-me um recibo se faz favor?**	
	dah-mə oong rəseeboo sə fahsh favawr	
Please forward my mail to...	**Pode fazer seguir a minha correspondência para...**	
	podə fazehr səgeer a meenya koorrəshpawngdehngseea para	
We have enjoyed ourselves very much.	**Divertimo-nos muito.**	
	deevərteemoo-noosh mooeengtoo	
May I have one of your leaflets?	**Dá-me um dos vossos folhetos?**	
	dah-mə oong doosh vosoosh foollyehtoosh	

Vocabulary

bar	**o bar**	oo bahr
barman	**o barman**	oo bahrman
bed	**a cama**	a kama
chair	**a cadeira**	a kadayra
chambermaid	**a empregada/a criada**	a ehngprəgahda/a kreeahda
children's playground	**o recreio**	oo rrəkrayoo

discotheque	a boite/a discoteca	a booahtə/a deeshkooteka
door	a porta	a porta
hall	a entrada	a ehngtrahda
lift	o elevador	oo eeləvadawr
light switch	o interruptor	oo eengtərrooptawr
lounge	a sala	a sahla
luggage porter	o porteiro	oo poortayroo
manager	o gerente	oo zherehngtə
radio	o rádio	oo rrahdeeoo
restaurant	o restaurante	oo rrəshtowrangtə
stairs	as escadas	ash əshkahdash
swimming pool	a piscina	a pəsheena
telephone operator	o (a) telefonista	oo (a) tələfooneeshta
waiter	o criado de mesa	oo kreeahdoo də mehza
waitress	a criada de mesa	a kreeahda də mehza
wardrobe	o armário	oo ahrmahreeoo
window	a janela	a zhanela

Catering for Yourself

Villas and Apartments

I have booked a villa/ an apartment.	**Aluguei uma casa/um apartamento.** aloogay ooma kahza/oong apartamehngtoo
Here is my voucher.	**Está aqui o meu talão.** əstah akee oo mehoo talowng
Will you please show me around?	**Podia-me mostrar a casa por favor?** poodeea-mə mooshtrahr a kahza poor favawr
Where is the light switch/power point/ fuse box?	**Onde é o interruptor/a ficha/os fusíveis?** awngde e oo eengtərrooptawr/a feesha/oosh foozeevaysh
Do all the outside doors lock?	**Há chave para todas as portas que dão para a rua?** ah shahvə para tawdash ash portash kə downg para a rrooa

How do the shutters work?	**Como é que funcionam as persianas?** kawmoo e kə foongseeawnang ash pərseeanash
Will you show me the hot water system?	**Podia-me mostrar o esquentador?** poodeea-mə mooshtrahr oo əshkehngtadawr
Where is the mains valve?	**Aonde é a válvula principal do gás?** aawngde e a vahlvoola preengseepahl doo gahsh
Are gas cylinders delivered?	**Vêm entregar o gás a casa?** vayehng ehngtrəgahr oo gahsh a kahza
Is there any domestic help?	**Há uma criada [empregada]?** ah ooma kreeahda [ehngprəgahda]
At what time does the house help come?	**A que horas vem a mulher a dias?** a kə orash vehng a moollyer a deeash
Can we have three sets of house keys?	**Arranja-nos chaves de casa para três pessoas?** arrangzha-noosh shahvəsh də kahza para trehsh pəsawash
When is the rubbish collected?	**Quando é que vêm buscar o lixo?** kooangdoo e kə vayehng booshkahr oo leeshoo
Are the shops nearby?	**Há lojas aqui perto?** ah lozhash akee pertoo
Where is the bus stop/ station?	**Onde é a paragem do autocarro/a estação?** awngde e a parahzhayng doo owtokahrroo/a əshtasowng
Have you a map of the area?	**Tem um mapa da região?** tehng oong mahpa da rrəzheeowng

Camping

Where can we camp for the night?	**Aonde é que podemos acampar hoje á noite?** aawngde e kə poodehmoosh akangpahr awzhə ah noytə
Have you got a site free?	**Tem espaço livre?** tehng əshpahsoo leevrə

Do you rent out	**Alugam**
	aloogang
bungalows?	**vivendas?**
	veevehngdash
tents?	**tendas?**
	tehngdash
cooking equipment?	**equipamento de cozinha?**
	eekeepamehngtoo de koozeenya
Are there toilet and washing facilities/ cooking facilities?	**Há casa de banho/uma cozinha?**
	ah kahza de banyoo/ooma koozeenya
How much does it cost per night?	**Quanto custa por noite?**
	kooangtoo kooshta poor noyta
Can I put my tent here?	**Posso armar a minha tenda aqui?**
	posoo armahr a meenya tehngda akee
May we put our caravan here?	**Podemos pôr a nossa rolote aqui?**
	podehmoosh pawr a nosa rroolota akee
Is there room for a trailer?	**Há espaço para um reboque?**
	ah əshpahsoo para oong rrəbokə
Is there a night guard?	**Tem guarda nocturno?**
	tehng gooahrda notoornoo
Where is	**Onde é**
	awngde e
the camp shop?	**a loja do parque?**
	a lozha doo pahrkə
the restaurant?	**o restaurante?**
	oo rrəshtowrangtə
the nearest shopping centre?	**o centro comercial mais próximo?**
	oo sehngtroo koomərseeahl mysh proseemoo
At what time do we have to vacate the site?	**A que horas é que temos que sair do parque?**
	a kə orash e kə tehmoosh kə saeer doo pahrkə
Where is the drinking water tap?	**Onde é a torneira de água potável?**
	awngde e a toornayra də ahgooa pootahvel

Vocabulary

barbecue	o churrasco	oo shoorrahshkoo
basin	o lavatório	oo lavatoreeoo
bucket	o balde	oo bahldə
camping gas	a bilha de gás	a beellya də gahsh
frame tent	a tenda com armação	a tehngda kawng ahrmasowng
grill	o grelhador	oo grəllyadawr
guy ropes	as cordas de firmar	ash kordash də feermahr
ice-bucket	o balde de gelo	oo bahldə də zhehloo
insecticide	o insecticida	oo eengseteeseeda
knife	a faca	a fahka
mosquito repellant	o mata moscas	oo mahta mawshkash
penknife	o canivete	oo kaneevetə
sleeping bag	o saco cama	oo sahkoo kama
spade	a pá	a pah
stove	o fogão	oo foogowng
tent	a tenda	a tehngda
tent peg	a cavilha	a kaveellya
waterproof sheet	o oleado	oo oleeahdoo

Youth Hostelling

Is there a youth hostel in this town?
Há um lar de estudantes nesta cidade?
ah oong lahr də əshtoodangtəsh **nesh**ta seed**ah**də

Have you room for tonight?
Tem lugar para hoje à noite?
tehng loogahr para awzhə ah noytə

What are the house rules?
Quais são as regras da casa?
kooysh sowng ash regrash da kahza

How long can we stay?
Quanto tempo podemos ficar?
kooangtoo tehngpoo poodehmoosh feekahr

Is there a youth hostel at...?
Há um lar de estudantes em...?
ah oong lahr də əshtoodangtəsh ayng

Eating and Drinking

Mealtimes offer not only the opportunity to satisfy the appetite but also provide an intimate glimpse of the lives of the people in the places you are visiting. Portuguese people like eating out, especially on Sundays when the whole family can be seen enjoying their Sunday lunch at restaurants and tascas. Usually the dishes are abundant and simply cooked, though given a rich flavour with a plentiful addition of herbs and olive oil.

When looking for a place to eat, remember that most hotels in tourist resorts will provide an international menu and if you want to eat local dishes you would do best to frequent pensões or tascas. Menus are displayed outside eating establishments and you can soon become practised at reading these with the help of your phrase book.

In Brazil the majority of restaurants serve international food but in every city there are one or two which offer Brazilian specialities. Seafood plays a big part in Brazilian cooking in which coconut milk or palm oil is often used as a cooking ingredient. Brazilians are also fond of barbecued steaks (churrascos) which come from their vast ranches in the south.

Can you recommend	**Pode recomendar**
	podə rrəkoomehngdahr
a good restaurant?	**um bom restaurante?**
	oong bawng rrəshtowrangtə
a restaurant that is not too expensive?	**um restaurante que não seja muito caro?**
	oong rrəshtowrangtə kə nowng sayzha **mooee**ngtoo kahroo
a typical restaurant of the region?	**um restaurante típico da região?**
	oong rrəshtowrangtə teepeekoo da rəzheeowng
Is there a good snack bar nearby?	**Há um bom snack-bar aqui perto?**
	ah oong bawng snack bar akee pertoo
Where can I find a self-service restaurant?	**Onde é que há um restaurante self-service aqui?**
	awngde e kə ah oong rrəshtowrangtə self-service akee
Do I need to reserve a table?	**É preciso marcar mesa?**
	e prəseezoo markahr mehza

I'd like a table for two	**Queria uma mesa para duas pessoas**
	kəreea ooma mehza para dooash pesawash
at nine o'clock.	**para as nove horas.**
	para ash novə orash
not too near the door.	**não muito próximo da porta.**
	nowng mooeengtoo proseemoo da porta
in the corner.	**no canto**
	noo kangtoo
away from the kitchen.	**longe da cozinha.**
	lawngzhə da koozeenya

At the Restaurant

A table for four, please.	**Uma mesa para quatro, por favor.**
	ooma mehza para kooahtroo poor favawr
Is this our table?	**É esta a nossa mesa?**
	e eshta a nosa mehza
This table will do fine.	**Esta mesa está óptima.**
	eshta mehza əshtah oteema
The tablecloth is dirty.	**A toalha está suja.**
	a tooahllya əshtah soozha
The table is unsteady.	**A mesa está desiquilibrada.**
	a mehza əshtah dəzeekəleebrahda
The ashtray is missing.	**Falta um cinzeiro.**
	fahlta oong seengzayroo
May I see the menu?	**Posso ver a lista?**
	posoo vehr a leeshta
We will have an aperitif while we look at the menu.	**Vamos tomar uma bebida enquanto escolhemos.**
	vamoosh toomahr ooma bəbeeda ehngkooangtoo əshkoollyehmoosh
Please bring the wine list.	**Se faz favor traz a lista dos vinhos?**
	sə fahsh favawr trahsh a leeshta doosh veenyoosh

Have you a set menu?	**Tem um menu fixo?** tehng oong mənoo feeksoo
What do you recommend today?	**O que é que aconselha para hoje?** oo kə e kə akawngsehllya para awzhə
What does it consist of?	**Como é feito este prato?** kawmoo e faytoo ehshtə prahtoo
It sounds good. I'll try it.	**Deve ser bom. Vou experimentar.** devə sehr bawng. vaw əshpəreemehngtahr
The soup is cold. Please warm it up.	**A sopa está fria. Podia mandar aquecer se faz favor?** a sawpa əshtah freea. poodeea mangdahr akesehr se fahsh favawr
This fork is dirty. May I have a clean one?	**Este garfo está sujo. Dá-me um limpo?** ehshtə gahrfoo əshtah soozhoo. dah-mə oong leengpòo
Will you call our waiter?	**Pode chamar o nosso criado?** podə shamahr oo nosoo kreeahdoo
We did not order this.	**Não pedimos isto.** nowng pədeemoosh eeshtoo
I'd like to speak to the head waiter.	**Queria falar com o chefe de mesa.** kəreea falahr kawng oo shefə də mehza
My compliments to the chef.	**Os meus parabens ao cozinheiro.** oosh mehoosh parabayngsh ow koozeenyayroo
It's very good.	**Está muito bom.** əshtah mooeengtoo bawng
Have you any house wine?	**Tem vinho da casa?** tehng veenyoo da kahza
I'd like a half bottle.	**Queria meia garrafa.** kəreea maya garrahfa
Which is the local wine?	**Qual é o vinho desta região?** kooahl e oo veenyoo deshta rrəzheeowng

This wine is corked.	**Este vinho sabe a rolha.**	
	ehshtə veenyoo sahbə a rrawllya	
The children will share a portion.	**As crianças comem um prato a meias.**	
	ash kreeangsash komayng oong prahtoo a mayash	
May we have some water?	**Trazia-nos água?**	
	trazeea-noosh ahgooa	
Have you any mineral water?	**Tem água mineral?**	
	tehng ahgooa meenərahl	
Have you a high chair for the child?	**Tem um cadeira alta para a criança?**	
	tehng ooma kadayra ahlta para a kreeangsa	
Would you please bring some cushions?	**Trazia umas almofadas se faz favor?**	
	trazeea oomash ahlmoofahdash se fahsh favawr	
Where are the toilets?	**Onde é a casa de banho?**	
	awngde e a kahza də banyoo	
May I have the bill, please?	**Dava-me a conta se fazia favor?**	
	dahva-mə a kawngta sə fazeea favawr	
Is service included?	**O serviço está incluido?**	
	oo sərveesoo əshtah eengklooeedoo	

Vocabulary

bill	**a conta**	a kawngta
boiled	**cozido**	koozeedoo
cheese	**a queijo**	oo kayzhoo
dessert	**a sobremesa**	a soobrəmehza
fish	**o peixe**	oo payshə
fork	**o garfo**	oo gahrfoo
fried	**frito**	freetoo
fruit	**a fruta**	a froota
glass	**o copo**	oo kopoo
grilled	**grelhado**	grəllyahdoo
knife	**a faca**	a fahka
meat	**a carne**	a kahrnə

medium	**médio**	medeeoo
menu	**a lista**	a leeshta
mustard	**a mostarda**	a mooshtahrda
napkin	**o guardanapo**	oo gooahrdanahpoo
oil	**o óleo/o azeite**	oo oleeoo/oo azaytə
omelet	**a omelete**	a oməletə
pepper	**a pimenta**	a peemehngta
rare	**mal passado**	mahl pasahdoo
roast	**assado**	asahdoo
salad	**a salada**	a salahda
salt	**o sal**	oo sahl
soft drink	**o refrigerante**	oo rrəfreezhərangtə
soup	**a sopa**	a sawpa
spoon	**a colher**	a koollyer
starter	**a entrada**	a ehngtrahda
stuffed	**recheado**	rrəsheeahdoo
sweet	**o doce**	oo dawsə
table	**a mesa**	a mehza
vegetables	**os legumes**	oosh ləgooməsh
vinegar	**o vinagre**	oo veenahgrə
water	**a água**	a ahgooa
well done	**bem passado**	bayng pasahdoo
wine	**o vinho**	oo veenyoo
wine list	**a lista dos vinhos**	a leeshta doosh veenyoosh

The Menu

The Portuguese like their food full of flavour, and as well as olive oil and garlic they use herbs freely and spices such as curry powder, which was first introduced by Henry the Navigator. Soups are a popular starter for a meal, and along the coast seafood is abundant and straight from the sea. Beef is plentiful, the sucking pig is delicious and there are other excellent pork products such as ham, tongue and sausages. And, of course, **bacalhau** or cod, the national dish of Portugal, offers 365 different recipes, one for each day of the year.

Restaurants offer fixed price and à la carte menus. The midday meal usually begins at noon and there is a long lunch hour; in the evening dinner begins at about 8.00 pm and often later.

In Brazil restaurant menus are derived from European styles of cooking but there are some exotic Brazilian dishes in which local tastes prevail. **Vatapa** is made of shrimps and fish with palm oil, **Sarapatel** of liver and heart with peppers and tomatoes, and **Feijoada** is the national stew, a kind of rich cassoulet.

Starters

anchovas	angshawvash	anchovies
croquetes de fiambre	kroketəsh də feeangbrə	cold meat croquettes
frituras de presunto	freetoorash də prezoongtoo	fried rolls of ham
limões de pescador	leemoyngsh də peshkadawr	lemons filled with sardines
rissois béchamel	rreesoeesh behshahmel	pastry rissoles
rissois de camarão	reesoeesh də kamarowng	shrimp rissoles
sardinhas	sardeenyash	sardines
tomates recheados	toomahtəsh rrəsheeahdoosh	stuffed tomatoes

Soups

caldo verde	kahldoo vehrdə	Portuguese cabbage soup (a speciality)
creme pastor	kremə pashtawr	shepherd's soup
gaspacho à Alentejana	gashpahshoo ah alehngtəzhana	Portuguese gazpacho with ham
sopa de marisco	sawpa də mareeshkoo	seafood soup
sopa de castanhas	sawpa də kashtanyash	chestnut soup

Fish

ameijoas à Espanhola	amayzhooash ah əshpanyola	clams Spanish style with peppers and tomatoes
ameijoas à Nazaré	amayzhooash ah nazare	clams Nazaré style with white wine and shallots
ameijoas à Portimão	amayzhooash ah poorteemowng	clams Portimão style with peppers and garlic
atum à Algarvia	atoong ah ahlgarveea	fresh tunny Algarve style
bacalhau à Biscainha	bakallyahoo ah beeshkaeenya	fried Biscay cod with tomatoes, peppers and potatoes
bacalhau dourado	bakallyahoo dawrahdoo	fried cod with tomatoes, peppers and garlic
caldeirada Nazaré	kahldayrahda nazare	fish stew Nazaré style
camarões com vinho do Porto	kamaroyngsh kawng veenyoo doo pawrtoo	prawns with port wine
conchas à bela aurora	kawngshash ah bela aoorora	crab in scallop shells
lagosta	lagawshta	lobster
lampreia	langpraya	sea lamprey
lulas de caldeirada	loolash də kahldayrahda	squid stew
ostras	awshtrash	oysters
pescada frita	pəshkahda freeta	fried hake
peixe espada	paysə əshpahda	swordfish
sardinhas no forno	sardeenyash noo fawrnoo	baked sardines

Meat

almondegas de carne	ahlmawngdəgash də kahrnə	meat balls

cabrito assado	kabreetoo asahdoo	roast kid
carne de porco à Alentejana	kahrnə de pawrkoo ah alehngtəzhana	pork in the Alentejana style with clams
cozido à Portuguesa	koozeedoo ah poortoogehza	beef and chicken stew
dobrada à Portuguesa	doobrahda ah poortoogehza	tripe with haricot beans
iscas à Portuguesa	eeshkash ah poortoogehza	liver in the Portuguese style
leitão	laytowng	sucking pig
lombo de porco	lawngboo də pawrkoo	loin of pork
miolos panados	meeoloosh panahdoosh	brains fried in breadcrumbs
porco com ameijoas	pawrkoo kawng amayzhooash	pork with clams
rim com arroz	reeng kawng arrawsh	kidneys with rice
rolo de carne	rawloo de kahrnə	meat-filled loaf
tripa à moda do Porto	treepa ah moda doo pawrtoo	tripe Oporto style with ham and chicken

Poultry and Game

coelho com arroz	kooəllyoo kawng arrawsh	rabbit with rice
frango com arroz	franggoo kawng arrawsh	chicken with rice
frango com ervilhas	franggoo kawng eerveellyash	chicken with peas
pato guisado	pahtoo geezahdoo	stewed duck
perdiz estufada	pərdeesh əshtoofahda	stuffed partridge
perú recheado com castanhas	pəroo rəsheeahdoo kawng kashtanyash	turkey stuffed with chestnuts

Vegetables

arroz açafrão	arrawsh asafrowng	saffron rice
arroz de tomate	arrawsh də toomahtə	tomato rice
batatas à Alentejana	batahtash ah alehngtezhana	Alentejo potatoes
batata doce	batahta dawsə	sweet potato
batatas gratinadas	batahtash grateenahdash	potatoes with cheese
berinjelas	bəreengzhelash	aubergines
brócolos à Portuguesa	brokooloosh ah poortoogehza	broccoli sautéed Portuguese style
ervilhas à Portuguesa	eerveellyash ah poortoogehza	Portuguese peas
favas à Ribatejana	fahvash ah reebatəzhana	broad beans Ribatejana style
pimentos fritos	peemehngtoosh freetoosh	fried peppers
puré de cebola	poore də səbawla	potato and onion puree
salada	salahda	salad

Desserts

arroz doce	arrawsh dawsə	creamed rice
bolas de figo	bolash də feegoo	fig balls
crepes à Portuguesa	krepəsh ah poortoogehza	Portuguese pancakes
doce de bolachas	dawsə də boolahshash	sweet biscuits
pudim flan	poodeeng flang	baked custard
rabanadas	rabanahdash	bread fritters
sonhos	sawnyoosh	fritters
sonhos de alperce	sawnyoosh də ahlpersə	apricot fritters
soufflé de castanhas	soofleh də kashtanyash	chestnut soufflé
tarte de amêndoa	tahrtə də amehngdooa	almond tart
toucinho do ceu	tawseenyoo doo seoo	'bacon from heaven' – a cake made from eggs, almonds and sugar

Drinks

Portugal is a wine-drinking country but also produces some excellent light lager-type beer. There is a varied mineral drink industry and bottled fruit juices come in many flavours. As in many Latin countries, it is the custom to drink natural mineral water at meals and Portugal has several renowned spas at Luso, Pedras Salgadas and Vidago. In the tourist resorts the usual international aperitifs and liqueurs are available.

Wine

The most famous of Portuguese wines is port which was created in the early eighteenth century to satisfy English tastes. Port comes from the Douro valley in northern Portugal and the industry is centred in Oporto. The next most famous wine associated with Portugal is Madeira which comes not from the mainland but from the island of that name. In recent years other Portuguese wines have become well known outside their country of origin, among them the **vinho verde** of the Minho and lower Douro valley. These are young, fresh wines and so are the sparkling rosé wines.

A more conventional type of wine is produced in the Dão area which lies in the centre of the country. Most of the Dão wines are red, full bodied and deep in colour.

Other Portuguese wine-growing areas are Alentejo, which produces a rich, strong wine; Colares, whose red wines are velvety and full bodied and Setubal, where a Muscatel is produced.

In Brazil, wine production is still in an early stage of development though good table wines are available. These come from the south of the country in the state of Rio Grande do Sul. There are also vineyards near São Paulo and Rio de Janeiro.

I'd like a glass of red wine/white wine, please.	**Queria um copo de vinho tinto/vinho branco, se faz favor.** kəreea oong kopoo də veenyoo teengtoo/veenyoo brangkoo se fahsh favawr

Is there a local wine? **Há algum vinho desta região?**
ah ahlgoong veenyoo deshta rrazheeowng

Two beers, please. **Duas cervejas, se faz favor.**
dooash sarvehzhash sa fahsh favawr

Have you any gin and **Tem gin tónico?**
tonic? tehng zheeng toneekoo

Some ice and lemon, **Gêlo e limão, por favor.**
please. zhehloo ee leemowng poor favawr

I'd like a Scotch with **Queria um whisky com gelo/com água lisa/com**
ice/with plain water/ **soda.**
with soda. kareea oong ooeeskee kawng zhehloo/kawng ahgooa
leeza/kawng soda

Have you any **Tem bebidas não alcoólicas?**
non-alcoholic drinks? tehng babeedash nowng ahlkoo-oleekash

VOCABULARY

beer	cerveja	servehzha
bottle	a garrafa	a garrahfa
brandy	brandy	brangdee
gin	gin	zheeng
glass	o copo	oo kopoo
lager	cerveja estrangeira	servehzha ashtrangzhayra
port	vinho do Porto	veenyoo doo pawrtoo
rum	rum	rroom
sherry	jerez	zharehsh
dry/medium/sweet	seco/médio/doce	sehkoo/medeeoo/ dawsa
soda	soda	soda
vermouth	vermoute	vermoota
vodka	vodka	vodka
whisky	whisky	ooeeskee

Soft Drinks

May we please have	**Por favor trazia-nos**
	poor favawr trazeea-noosh
a pot of tea?	**um bule de chá?**
	oong boolə də shah
a lemon tea?	**um chá de limão?**
	oong shah də leemowng
a coffee with milk/ cream/ sugar?	**um café com leite/ natas/ açúcar?**
	oong kafe kawng laytə/ nahtash/ asookar
a black coffee?	**um café (uma bica)?**
	oong kafe (ooma beeka)
an iced coffee?	**um mazagran?**
	oong mahzahgrang
Have you any lemonade?	**Tem limonada?**
	tehng leemoonahda
I'd like	**Queria**
	kəreea
an orange juice with soda water.	**um sumo de laranja com soda**
	oong soomoo də larangzha kawng soda
a glass of cold milk.	**um copo de leite frio.**
	oong kopoo də laytə freeoo
I'd like a cool drink with plenty of ice.	**Queria uma bebida fresca com muito gelo.**
	kəreea ooma bəbeeda frehshka kawng mooeengtoo zhehloo
Have you a straw?	**Tem uma palhinha?**
	tehng ooma pallyeenya
Do you make milk shakes?	**Fazem batidos?**
	fahzayng bateedoosh
Have you a bottle with a screw top?	**Tem uma garrafa com tampa de enroscar?**
	tehng ooma garrahfa kawng tangpa də ehngrrooshkahr

VOCABULARY

beeftea	Bovril	bovreel
chocolate	o chocolate	oo shookoolahtə
cordial	o cordial/o tónico	oo kordeeahl/oo toneekoo
cup	a chávena	a shahvəna
fruit juice	o sumo de fruta	oo soomoo də froota
ginger ale	o ginger ale	oo ginger ale
lemon	o limão	oo leemawng
lime juice	o sumo de lima	oo soomoo də leema
mineral water	a água mineral	a ahgooa meenərahl
orange	a laranja	a larangzha
syphon	o sifão	oo seefowng
tonic	a água tónica	a ahgooa toneeka
tumbler	o copo	oo kopoo

Shopping

Buying Food

Eating out is fun, but so is buying Portuguese food in the various types of food shops and markets. The Portuguese set great store by freshness and quality, and buying food is an important operation involving much discussion about the product.

At the Butcher's

What kind of meat is that?	**Que género de carne é essa?** kə zheneroo də **kahrnə·e** esa
What do you call that cut?	**Como é que se chama essa peça de carne?** kawmoo e kə sə shama esa pesa də **kahrnə**
I'd like some steaks, please.	**Queria uns bifes, se faz favor.** kəreea oongsh beefəs sə fahsh favawr
How much does that weigh?	**Quanto é que pesa?** kooangtoo e kə peza
Will you please trim off the fat?	**Podia aparar a gordura, se faz favor?** poodeea aparahr a goordoora sə fahsh favawr
Will you take the meat off the bone?	**Podia tirar o osso?** poodeea teerahr oo awsoo
Will you mince it?	**Podia picá-la?** poodeea peekah-la
Please cut it in thin slices/ in thick slices.	**Se faz favor corte-a em fatias finas/ fatias grossas.** sə fahsh favawr kortee a ayng fateeash feenash/ fateeash grosash
Will you chine the cutlets?	**Pode cortar as costeletas?** podə koortahr ash kooshtelehtash

I'll have a little more.	**Dava-me mais um bocado?**	
	dahva-mə mysh oong bookahdoo	
That's too much.	**Isso é demais.**	
	eesoo e dəmysh	
Please put it in a plastic bag.	**Podia pôr num saco de plástico se faz favor?**	
	poodeea pawr noong sahkoo də plahshteekoo se fahsh favawr	
Cut it in cubes, please.	**Podia cortar em cubos, se faz favor.**	
	poodeea koortahr ayng kooboosh sə fahsh favawr	

VOCABULARY

bacon	**o bacon**	oo bacon
beef	**carne de vaca**	kahrnə də vahka
steak	**o bife**	oo beefə
stewing beef	**a carne de guisar**	a kahrnə də geezahr
brains	**os miolos**	oosh meeoloosh
butcher	**o talho**	oo tahllyoo
cooking fat	**a banha**	a banya
cutlets	**as costeletas**	ash kooshtəlehtash
escalope	**o escalope**	oo əshkalopə
kidneys	**os rins**	oosh reengsh
lamb cutlets	**as costeletas de carneiro**	ash kooshtelehtash de karnayroo
lamb, leg of	**a perna de carneiro**	a perna də karnayroo
lamb, shoulder of	**a pá de carneiro**	a pah də karnayroo
liver	**o fígado**	oo feegadoo
pigs' trotters	**o chispe**	oo sheeshpə
pork chops	**as costeletas de porco**	ash kooshtəlehtash də pawrkoo
pork, knuckle of	**o jarrete**	oo zharrehtə
pork, leg of	**a perna de porco**	a perna də pawrkoo
sausage	**a salsicha**	a sahlseesha
sweetbreads	**as miudezas**	ash meeoodehzash
tongue	**a língua**	a leenggooa

At the Fishmonger's

Will you clean the fish?	**Podia arranjar o peixe?** poodeea arrangzhahr oo payshə
Please take off the head/ the tail/ the fins.	**Podia cortar a cabeça/ o rabo/ as barbatanas.** poodeea koortahr a kabehsa/ oo rrahboo/ ash barbatanash
Have you any shell fish?	**Tem marisco?** tehng mareeshkoo
What is the name of that fish?	**Como é que se chama esse peixe?** kawmoo e kə sə shama ehsə payshə

VOCABULARY

anchovies	**as anchovas**	ash angshawvash
bass	**o robalo**	oo rroobahloo
bream	**o sargo**	oo sahrgoo
carp	**a carpa**	a karpa
clam	**a ameijoa**	a amayzhooa
cod	**o bacalhau**	oo bakallyow
crab	**a santola**	a sangtola
crayfish	**o lagostim**	oo lagooshteeng
eel	**a enguia**	a ehngeea
fishmonger's shop	**a peixaria**	a payshareea
herring	**o arenque**	oo arehngkə
lobster	**a lagosta**	a lagawshta
mullet	**o salmonete**	oo sahlmoonehtə
mussel	**o mexilhão**	oo məsheellyowng
octopus	**o polvo**	oo pawlvoo
oysters	**as ostras**	ash awshtrash
perch	**a perca**	a perka
pike	**o lúcio**	oo looseeoo
plaice	**a solha**	a sawllya
prawn	**o camarão**	oo kamarowng
salmon	**o salmão**	oo sahlmowng

sardine	**a sardinha**	a sardeenya
sole	**o linguado**	oo leenggooahdoo
squid	**a lula**	a loola
trout	**a truta**	a troota
tunny	**o atum**	oo atoong
turbot	**o pregado**	oo prəgahdoo
whitebait	**o joaquimzinho**	oò zhooakeengzeenyoo

At the Delicatessen/Grocer

What kinds of sausage have you got?	**Que enchidos é que têm?** kə enhgsheedoosh e kə tayehng
I'd like	**Queria** kəreea
a mild one/a peppery one/one without garlic.	**um não muito picante/um picante/um sem alho.** oong nowng mooeengtoo peekangtə/oong peekangtə/oong sayng ahllyoo
What kinds of pâté have you?	**Que pâtés é que têm?** kə pahtehsh e kə tayehng
I prefer a coarse pâté/smooth pâté/game pâté.	**Prefiro pâté grosso/pâté em pasta/pâté de caça.** prəfeeroo pahteh grawsoo/pahteh ayng pahshta/pahteh də kahsa
What is the name of that cheese?	**Como é que se chama esse queijo?** kawmoo e kə sə shama ehsə kayzhoo
Have you any goat's cheese?	**Tem queijo de cabra?** tehng kayzhoo də kahbra
Do I have to take the whole cheese or will you cut me a piece?	**Tenho que comprar o queijo inteiro ou pode-me cortar um bocado?** tenyoo kə kawngprahr oo kayzhoo ehngtayroo aw podə-mə koortahr oong bookahdoo
May I test it for ripeness?	**Posso ver se está bem curado?** posoo vehr sə əshtah bayng koorahdoo

Do you sell breakfast cereals?	**Vendem cereais para o pequeno-almoço [o café da manhã]?**	
	vehngdayng serreeysh para oo pəkehnoo ahlmawsoo [oo kafe da manyang]	
Have you any sweet biscuits/plain biscuits/ water biscuits?	**Tem bolachas doces/bolachas simples/bolachas de água e sal?**	
	tehng boolahshash dawsəsh/boolahshash seengpləsh/ boolahshash də ahgooa ee sahl	
I'll take a little of each salad.	**Queria um bocado de cada salada.**	
	kəreea oong bookahdoo də kada salahda	
Have you a tube of tomato purée?	**Tem um tubo de concentrado de tomate?**	
	tehng oong tooboo də kawngsehngtrahdoo də toomahtə	
I would like a jar of olives.	**Queria um frasco de azeitonas.**	
	kəreea oong frahshkoo də azaytawnash	

VOCABULARY

bacon	**o bacon**	oo bakon
biscuits	**as bolachas**	ash boolahshash
bread	**o pão**	oo powng
brush	**a escova**	a əshkawva
butter	**a manteiga**	a mangtayga
cereals	**os cereais**	oosh serreeysh
cheese	**o queijo**	oo kayzhoo
chocolate	**o chocolate**	oo shookoolahtə
cleaning fluid	**o produto de limpeza**	oo proodootoo də leengpehza
coffee	**o café**	oo kafe
crisps	**as batatas fritas**	ash batahtash freetash
detergent	**o detergente**	oo dətərzhengtə
disinfectant	**o desinfectante**	oo dəseengfetangtə
dried fruit	**a fruta cristalisada**	a froota kreestaleezahda
duster	**o pano do pó**	oo panoo doo po
eggs	**os ovos**	oosh ovoosh

flour	a farinha	a fareenya
garlic sausage	o chouriço	oo shawreesoo
grocer's shop	a mercearia	a mərseeareea
ham	o fiambre [o presunto]	oo feeangbrə [oo prəsoongtoo]
herbs	as ervas aromáticas	ash ervash aroomahteekash
jam	a compota	a kawngpota
macaroni	o macarrão	oo makarrowng
margarine	a margarina	a margareena
matches	os fósforos	oosh foshfooroosh
milk	o leite	oo laytə
mustard	a mostarda	a mooshtahrda
oil	o óleo/o azeite	oo oleeoo/oo azaytə
olives	as azeitonas	ash azaytawnash
paper napkins	os guardanapos de papel	oosh gooahrdanahpoosh də papel
pepper	a pimenta	a peemehngta
pickles	os pickles	oosh peekləsh
rice	o arroz	oo arrawsh
salt	o sal	oo sahl
smoked fish	o peixe fumado	oo payshə foomahdoo
spaghetti	o espárguete	oo əshpahrgetə
sugar	o açúcar	oo asookar
tea	o chá	oo shah
tinned food	a comida em lata	a koomeeda ayng lahta
vinegar	o vinagre	oo veenahgrə
washing powder	o detergente	oo dətərzhehngtə

Cheeses

cabreiro	cabrayroo	goat's cheese
queijo da serra	kayzhoo da serra	creamy semi-hard cheese
queijo de Azeitão	kayzhoo də azaytowng	cream cheese
queijo do Alentejo	kayzhoo doo alehngtehzhoo	flavourful cheese from southern Portugal

rabaçal	rabasahl	a goat's cheese from the Pombal region.

At the Greengrocer and Fruiterer's

Is the melon ripe?	**O melão está maduro?**
	oo məlowng əshtah madooroo

How many will make a kilo?	**Quantos (quantas) fazem um quilo?**
	kooangtoosh (kooangtash) fahzayng oong keeloo

It's for eating today/tomorrow.	**É para comer hoje/amanhã.**
	e para koomehr awzhə/ahmanyang

Will you please weigh this?	**Podia pesar isto se faz favor?**
	podeea pəzahr eeshtoo sə fahsh favawr

This lettuce is rather limp.	**Esta alface está um bocado murcha.**
	eshta ahlfahsə əshtah oong bookahdoo moorsha

Are these apples crisp?	**Estas maçãs são frescas?**
	eshtash masangsh sowng frehshkash

I will put it in my carrier.	**Vou pôr no meu saco.**
	vaw pawr noo mehoo sahkoo

Have you got a box?	**Tem uma caixa?**
	tehng ooma kysha

VOCABULARY

almonds	**as amêndoas**	ash amehngdooash
apples	**as maçãs**	ash masangsh
apricots	**os alperces [os damascos]**	oosh ahlpersəsh [oosh damahshkoosh]
artichoke	**a alcachofra**	a ahlkashofra
asparagus	**os espargos**	oosh əshpahrgoosh
aubergines	**as beringelas**	ash bəreengzhelash
avocados	**as peras abacate**	ash pehrash abakahtə

bananas	as bananas	ash bananash
beans, broad	as favas	ash fahvash
French	o feijão verde	oo fayzhowng vehrdə
runner	o feijão	oo fayzhowng
beetroot	a beterraba	a bətərrahba
blackberries	as amoras	ash amorash
broccoli	os brócolos	oosh brokooloosh
cabbage	a couve	a kawvə
carrots	as cenouras	ash sənawrash
cauliflower	a couve-flor	a kawvə-flawr
celery	o aipo	oo ypoo
cherry	a cereja	a serehzha
chestnuts	as castanhas	ash kashtanyash
courgettes	as courgettes	ash koorzhetəsh
cress	os agriões	oosh agreeoyngsh
cucumber	o pepino	oo pəpeenoo
dates	as tâmaras	ash tamarash
figs	os figos	oosh feegoosh
garlic	o alho	oo allyoo
grapefruit	a toranja	a toorangzha
grapes	as uvas	ash oovash
greengages	as rainhas cláudias	ash rraeenyash klowdeeash
hazelnuts	as avelãs	ash avəlangsh
leeks	os alhos porros	oosh allyoosh pawrroosh
lemons	os limões	oosh leemoyngsh
lettuce	a alface	a ahlfahsə
melon	o melão	oo məlowng
mushrooms	os cogumelos	oosh koogoomeloosh
nuts	as nozes	ash nozəsh
onions	as cebolas	ash səbawlash
oranges	as laranjas	ash larangzhash
peaches	os pêssegos	oosh pehsəgoosh
pears	as peras	ash pehrash
peas	as ervilhas	ash eerveellyash
pineapple	o ananás [o abacaxís]	oo ananash [oo abahasheesh]
plums	as ameixas	ash amayshash
potatoes	as batatas	ash batahtash

radishes	**os rabanetes**	oosh rrabanehtəsh
raspberries	**as framboesas**	ash frangboooehzash
rhubarb	**o ruibarbo**	oo rooeebahrboo
strawberries	**os morangos**	oosh mooranggoosh
sweet corn	**o milho**	oo meellyoo
sweet pepper	**o pimento**	oo peemehngtoo
tangerines	**as tangerinas**	ash tangzhəreenash
tomatoes	**os tomates**	oosh toomahtəsh
turnips	**os nabos**	oosh nahboosh

Other Shops

Portuguese towns and villages are full of shops run by individual shopkeepers. This makes shopping a pleasure for its variety as well as for the unique character of each establishment. Most shops are open from 8.30 to 13.00 and from 15.00 to 19.00 and even later in the summer. In Brazil shops are usually open from 8.00 to 18.00. In both countries shops are generally closed on Saturday afternoon.

I want to go shopping.	**Quero ir às compras.**
	keroo eer ahsh kawngprash
Where are	**Aonde é que são**
	aawngde e kə sowng
the best shops?	**as melhores lojas?**
	ash mellyorəsh lozhash
the most popular shops?	**as lojas mais populares?**
	ash lozhash mysh poopoolahrəsh
the cheapest shops?	**as lojas mais baratas?**
	ash lozhash mysh barahtash
Where is the market?	**Aonde é que é o mercado (a praça)?**
	aawngde e kə e oo mərkahdoo (a prahsa)
Till what time are you open?	**Até que horas é que ficam abertos?**
	ate kə orash e kə feekang abertoosh
Is there a grocer's near here?	**Há uma mercearia aqui perto?**
	ah ooma mərseeareea akee pertoo

VOCABULARY

antique shop	o antiquário	ooo angteekooahreeoo
art gallery	a galeria de arte	a galəreea də ahrtə
baker's shop	a padaria	a pahdareea
beauty salon	o salão de beleza	oo salowng də bəlehza
bookshop	a livraria	a leevrareea
butcher's shop	o talho	oo tahllyoo
chemist's shop	a farmácia	a farmahseea
confectionery	a pastelaria	a pashtəlareea
dairy	a leitaria	a laytareea
delicatessen	a charcuteria	a sharkootəreea
department store	o armazém	oo ahrmazayng
dry cleaner	a limpeza a seco	a leengpehza a sehkoo
fishmonger's shop	a peixaria	a payshareea
greengrocer's shop	a loja de hortaliça	a lozha də ortaleesa
grocer's shop	a mercearia	a mərseeareea
hairdresser	o cabeleireiro	oo kabəlayrayroo
hardware store	a loja de ferragens	a lozha də fərrahzhayngsh
jeweller	o ourives	oo awr̃ ɛvəsh
newsagent	a tabacaria	a tabakareea
optician	o oculista	oo okooleeshta
photographer's	o fotógrafo	oo footografoo
shoemaker	o sapateiro	oo sapatayroo
shoe shop	a sapataria	a sapatareea
stationery shop	a papelaria	a papəlareea
supermarket	o supermercado	oo soopermərkahdoo
tailor	o alfaiate	oo ahlfaeeahtə
tobacconist's shop	a tabacaria	a tabakareea
toy shop	a loja de brinquedos	a lozha də breengkehdoosh
travel agency	a agência de viagens	a azhehngseea də veeahzhayngsh
watchmaker	o relojoeiro	oo rəloozhooayroo
wine merchant's	a loja de vinhos	a lozha də veenyoosh

Buying Clothes

I am just looking, thank you	**Estou só a ver, obrigado(a)** əshtaw so a vehr obreegahdoo(a)
I would like to look at	**Gostaria de ver** gooshtareea də vehr
some shirts.	**umas camisas.** oomash kameezash
plain shirts.	**camisas lisas.** kameezash leezash
coloured shirts.	**camisas de côr.** kameezash de kawr
striped shirts.	**camisas às riscas.** kameezash ahsh rreeshkash
cotton shirts.	**camisas de algodão.** kameezash də ahlgoodowng
shirts with long/short sleeves.	**camisas de manga comprida/curta.** kameezash de mangga kawngpreeda/koorta
My size is...	**O meu tamanho é o...** oo mehoo tamanyoo e oo
My collar size is...	**O tamanho do colarinho é o...** oo tamanyoo doo koolareenyoo e oo
This colour does not suit me.	**Esta côr não me fica bem.** eshta kawr nowng mə feeka bayng
Have you something in red/ in wool?	**Tem em encarnado [vermelho] / em lã?** tehng ayng ehngkarnahdoo [vermehllyoo] / ayng lang
I want something more casual.	**Quero uma coisa mais prática.** keroo ooma koyza mysh prahteeka
Is there a fitting room where I can try it on?	**Há uma sala aonde possa provar?** ah ooma sahla aawngdə posa proovahr
Can I return it if it is unsuitable?	**Posso devolver se não ficar bem?** posoo dəvolvehr sə nowng feekahr bayng

May I have a receipt?	**Dava-me um recibo?**	
	dahva-mə oong rrəseeboo	
It does not fit. It is too large/small/narrow/wide.	**Não me serve. É grande demais/pequeno demais/ apertado demais/largo demais.**	
	nowng mə servə. e grangdə dəmysh/pəkehnoo dəmysh/ apərtahdoo dəmysh/lahrgoo dəmysh	
Can you show me something else?	**Podia-me mostrar outra coisa?**	
	poodeea-mə mooshtrahr awtra koyza	
The zip is stuck/ broken.	**O fecho éclair está preso/partido.**	
	oo fayshoo eekler əshtah prehzoo/parteedoo	

VOCABULARY

MATERIALS

camel hair	o pelo de camelo	oo pehloo də kamehloo
chiffon	o chifon	oo sheefawng
cotton	o algodão	oo ahlgoodowng
crepe	o crepe	oo krepə
denim	a ganga	a gangga
felt	o feltro	oo fehltroo
flannel	a flanela	a flanela
gabardine	a gabardine	a gahbahrdeenə
lace	a renda	a rehngda
leather	o cabedal	oo kabədahl
linen	o linho	oo leenyoo
nylon	o nylon	oo nylon
piqué	o piqué	oo peekeh
poplin	a popelina	a popəleena
rayon	a seda vegetal	a sehda vəzhətahl
satin	o setim	oo səteeng
silk	a seda	a sehda
suede	a camurça	a kamoorsa
taffeta	o tafetá	oo tafətah
tweed	o tweed	oo tweed

velour	**o veludilho**	oo vəloodeellyoo
velvet	**o veludo**	oo vəloodoo
wool	**a lã**	a lang
worsted	**o estambre**	oo əshtangbrə

MEASUREMENTS

arm	**o braço**	oo brahsoo
chest	**o peito**	oo paytoo
hip	**a anca**	a angka
leg	**a perna**	a perna
length	**o comprimento**	oo kawngpreemehngtoo
neck	**o pescoço**	oo pəshkawsoo
waist	**a cintura**	a seengtoora

COLOUR

beige	**beige**	bezhə
black	**preto**	prehtoo
blue	**azul**	azool
brown	**castanho [marron]**	kashtanyoo [mahrrawng]
green	**verde**	vehrdə
mauve	**lilás**	leelahsh
orange	**côr de laranja**	kawr de larangzha
pastel colours	**cores claras**	kawrəsh klahrash
red	**encarnado [vermelho]**	ehngkarnahdoo [vərmehllyoo]
rose	**côr de rosa**	kawr də roza
strong colours	**côres vivas**	kawrəsh veevash
violet	**violeta**	veeoolehta
white	**branco**	brangkoo
yellow	**amarelo**	amareloo

ITEMS OF CLOTHING

anorak	**o anoraque**	oo anorahkə
bathing hat	**a touca de banho**	a tawka də banyoo
bathrobe	**o roupão**	oo rrawpowng

belt	o cinto	oo seengtoo
blazer	o blazer	oo blayzər
blouse	a blusa	a blooza
boots	as botas	ash botash
bra	o soutien	oo sooteeang
briefs	as cuecas	ash kooekash
buckle	a fivela	a feevela
button	o botão	oo bootowng
cap	o boné	oo bone
cardigan	o casaco de malha	oo kazahkoo də mahllya
coat	o casaco	oo kazahkoo
dinner jacket	o smoking	oo smokeeng
dress	o vestido	oo vəshteedoo
dressing gown	o roupão [o robe]	oo rrawpowng [oo rrobə]
elastic	o elástico	oo eelahshteekoo
girdle	a cinta	a seengta
gloves	as luvas	ash loovash
gym shoes	os sapatos de ténis	oosh sapahtoosh də teneesh
handkerchief	o lenço	oo lehngsoo
hat	o chapéu	oo shapeoo
hook and eyes	o colchete	oo kolshehtə
jacket	o casaco [o paletó]	oo kazahkoo [oo palətó]
jeans	as jeans/as calças de ganga	ash jeans/ash kahlsash də ganga
jumper	a camisola [o pullover]	a kameezola [oo poolovər]
négligé	a camisa de noite e roupão	a kameeza de noytə ee rrawpowng
nightdress	a camisa de noite	a kameeza də noytə
overcoat	o casacão/o sobretudo	oo kazakowng/oo sawbretoodoo
panties	as cuecas	ash kooekash
pants suit	o fato [o terno]	oo fahtoo [oo ternoo]
pocket	a algibeira [o bolso]	a ahlzheebayra [oo bawlsoo]
press stud	o botão de colarinho	oo bootowng də koolareenyoo

pullover	a camisola [o pullover]	a kameezola [oo poolovər]
pyjamas	o pijama	oo peezhama
raincoat	a capa de chuva/a gabardine	a kahpa də shoova/a gabahrdeenə
sandals	as sandálias.	ash sangdahleeash
scarf	o lenço	oo lehngsoo
shirt	a camisa	a kameeza
shoelaces	os atacadores	oosh atakadawrəsh
shoes	os sapatos	oosh sapahtoosh
shorts	os calções	oosh kalsoyngsh
skirt	a saia	a sya
slip	a saia de baixo	a sya də byshoo
slippers	os chinelos	oosh sheeneloosh
socks	as meias	ash mayash
stockings	as meias de seda	ash mayash də sehda
suit	o fato [o terno]	oo fahtoo [oo ternoo]
suspenders	a cinta de ligas	a seengta də leegash
swimsuit	o fato de banho	oo fahtoo də banyoo
thread	a linha	a leenya
tie	a gravata	a gravahta
tights	os collants	oosh kolangsh
trousers	as calças	ash kahlsash
T-shirt	a T-shirt	a T-shirt
twinset	o conjunto de malha	oo kawngzhoongtoo de mahllya
underpants	as cuecas	ash kooekash
vest	a camisola interior	a kameezola eengtəreeawr
waistcoat	o colete	oo koolehtə
zip	o fecho éclair	oo fayshoo eekler

At the Shoe Shop

I want a pair of	Quero um par de
	keroo oong pahr də
walking shoes.	sapatos normais.
	sapahtoosh normysh
evening shoes.	sapatos para a noite.
	sapahtoosh para a noytə

moccasins.	**mocasins.**	
	mokasangsh	
boots.	**botas.**	
	botash	
suede shoes.	**sapatos de camurça.**	
	sapahtoosh də kamoorsa	
slippers.	**chinelos.**	
	sheeneloosh	
sandals.	**sandálias.**	
	sangdahleeash	
canvas shoes.	**sapatos de ténis.**	
	sapahtoosh de teneesh	

My size is...

O meu tamanho é o...
oo mehoo tamanyoo e oo

I would like shoes with a broad/ narrow fitting.

Queria sapatos largos/ apertados
kəreea sapahtoosh lahrgoosh/apertahdoosh

I would like shoes with

Queria sapatos com
kəreea sapahtoosh kawng

high heels.	**saltos altos.**	
	sahltoosh ahltoosh	
low heels.	**saltos baixos.**	
	sahltoosh byshoosh	
leather soles.	**solas de cabedal.**	
	solash də kabədahl	
rubber soles.	**solas de borracha.**	
	solash də boorrahsha	
cork soles.	**solas de cortiça.**	
	solash də koorteesa	

These are not comfortable.

Estes não são confortáveis.
ehshtəsh nowng sowng kawngfoortahvaysh

May I try the other shoe?

Posso experimentar o outro sapato?
posoo əshpəreemehngtahr oo awtroo sapahtoo

Have you got a shoe horn?

Tem uma calçadeira?
tehng ooma kahlsadayra?

They are not my style.	**Não são o meu género.** nowng sowng oo mehoo zhenəroo
What other colours have you got?	**Que outras côres é que tem?** kə awtrash kawrəsh e kə tehng
How much are they?	**Quanto é que custam?** kooangtoo e kə kooshtang
That is more than I want to pay.	**Isso é mais do que eu quero pagar.** eeso e mysh doo kə ehoo keroo pagahr
I will wear them. Will you please wrap up my old shoes?	**Levo-os já calçados. Podia embrulhar os meus sapatos velhos por favor?** lehvoo-oosh zhah kahlsahdoosh. poodeea ehngbroollyahr oosh mehoosh sapahtoosh vellyoosh poor favawr
Do you sell shoe polish/shoebrushes?	**Vendem graxa/escovas para limpar sapatos?** vehngdayng grahsha/əshkawvash para leengpahr sapahtoosh

Tobacconist's

Do you sell English/ American cigarettes?	**Vendem cigarros inglêses/americanos?** vehngdayng seegahrroosh eengglehzəsh/aməreekanoosh
Have you any filter tip/king-size/ menthol-cooled cigarettes?	**Tem cigarros com filtro/cigarros king-size/ cigarros de mentol?** tehng seegahrroosh kawng feeltroo/seegahrroosh king-size/seegahrroosh də mehngtol
Do you sell pipe tobacco?	**Vendem tabaco para cachimbo?** vehngdayng tabahkoo para kăsheengboo
May I see your selection of pipes?	**Posso ver a vossa selecção de cachimbos?** posoo vehr a vosa səleksowng də kasheengboosh
I'd like a cigar.	**Queria um charuto.** kəreea oong sharootoo.

A packet/a carton of cigarettes please.	**Um maço/um pacote de cigarros, se faz favor.**	oong mahsoo/oong pakotə də seegahrroosh sə fahsh favawr
A box of matches, please.	**Uma caixa de fósforos por favor.**	ooma kysha də foshfooroosh poor favawr
Have you a cigar cutter?	**Tem um corta-charutos?**	tehng oong korta-sharootoosh
Do you sell pipe cleaners?	**Vendem limpadores de cachimbo?**	vehngdayng leengpadawrəsh də kasheengboo

Vocabulary

carton	**o pacote**	oo pakotə
case	**a cigarreira**	a seegarrayra
cigarette lighter	**o isqueiro**	oo eeshkayroo
flint	**a pedra**	a pedra
gas	**o gás**	oo gahsh
lighter fluid	**a gasolina**	a gazooleena
matches	**os fósforos**	oosh foshfooroosh
packet	**o maço**	oo mahsoo
pipe	**o cachimbo**	oo kasheengboo
pipe-cleaner	**o limpador de cachimbos**	oo leengpadawr də kasheengboosh
pouch	**o saco de cachimbo**	oo sahkoo də kasheengboo

Hardware Stores and Electrical Goods

I'd like a saucepan/a frying pan.	**Queria um tacho/uma frigideira.**	kəreea oong tahshoo/ooma freezheedayra
Have you a grill/any charcoal?	**Tem um grelhador [fogareiro] / carvão?**	tehng oong grəllyadawr [foogarayroo] / karvowng

I need a plastic bucket/ a metal bucket.	**Preciso de um balde de plástico/um balde de metal.** prəseezoo də oong **bahldə** də **plahshteekoo**/oong **bahldə** de mətahl	
Give me a ball of strong twine, please.	**Dava-me um rolo de cordel resistente, por favor.** dahva-mə oong **rrawloo** də koordel rrəzeeshtehngtə poor favawr	
I need a tow rope and a hook.	**Preciso de uma corda de reboque e um gancho.** prəseezoo də ooma korda də rrəbokə ee oong gangshoo	
I need a battery for my torch/ my radio.	**Preciso de uma pilha para a minha lanterna/ o meu rádio.** prəseezoo də ooma peellya para a meenya langterna/ oo mehoo rahdeeoo	
Can you repair this?	**Pode arranjar isto?** podə arrangzhahr eeshtoo	

VOCABULARY

adaptor	o transformador	oo trangshfoormadawr
basket	o cesto	oo sehshtoo
battery	a pilha	a peellya
brush	a escova	a əshkawva
bulb	a lâmpada	a langpada
car radio	o rádio do carro	oo rrahdeeoo doo kahrroo
chamois leather	a camurça	a kamoorsa
distilled water	a água distilada	a ahgooa dəshteelahda
fork	o garfo	oo gahrfoo
hammer	o martelo	oo marteloo
insulating tape	a fita isoladora	a feeta eezooladawra
iron	o ferro de engomar	oo ferroo də ehnggoomahr
kettle	a chaleira	a shalayra
knife	a faca	a fahka
mallet	o malho	oo mahllyoo
penknife	o canivete	oo kaneevetə

percolator	a máquina de café	a mahkeena de kafe
saw	a serra	a serra
scissors	a tesoura	a təzawra
screwdriver	a chave de parafusos	a shahvə də parafoozoosh
shaver	a plaina	a plyna
spoon	a colher	a koollyer
string	o cordel	oo koordel
tweezers	as pinças	ash peengsash
wire	o arame	oo aramə
wrench	a chave de porcas	a shahvə də porkash

Chemist

Do I need a doctor's prescription?	Preciso de receita médica?	prəseezoo də rrəsayta medeeka
Is there an all-night chemist open?	Há uma farmácia de serviço aberta toda a noite?	ah ooma farmahseea də sərveesoo aberta tawda a noytə
Can you make up this prescription?	Pode-me aviar esta receita?	podə-mə aveeahr eshta rrəsayta
When will it be ready?	Quando é que está pronto?	kooangdoo e kə əshtah prawngtoo
Will you write down the instructions? In English, if possible.	Pode-me escrever as instruções? Em inglês se for possível.	podə-mə əshkrəvehr ash eengshtroosoyngsh. ayng eengglehsh se fawr pooseevel
Is this suitable for children?	Isto serve para crianças?	eeshtoo servə para kreeangsash
Have you anything for	Tem qualquer coisa para	tehng kooahlker koyza para
a cold?	a constipação [o resfriamento]?	a kawngshteepasowng [oo rreshfreeamehngtoo]

Have you anything for	**Tem qualquer coisa para** tehng kooahlker koyza para
a sore throat?	**as dores de garganta?** ash dawrəsh də gargangta
a cough?	**a tose?** a tosə
I'd like to buy a thermometer.	**Queria comprar um termómetro** kəreea kawngprahr oong tərmometroo
Would you please have a look at this cut/bruise?	**Podia examinar este corte/esta nódoa negra mancha roxa, por favor?** poodeea eezameenahr ehshtə kortə/eshta nodooa nehgra mangsha rrawsha poor favawr
What kind of bandage would be best?	**Que género de ligadura seria a melhor?** kə genəroo də leegadoora səreea a məllyor
I've got	**Estou com** əshtaw kawng
indigestion.	**indigestão.** eengdəzhəshtowng
diarrhoea.	**diarreia.** deearraya
a headache.	**dores de cabeça.** dawrəsh də kabehsa
an upset stomach.	**dores de barriga.** dawrəsh də barreega
sunburn.	**queimaduras de sol.** kaymadoorash də sol
I am constipated.	**Estou com prisão de ventre.** əshtaw kawng preezowng də vehngtrə

VOCABULARY

MEDICINES

antibiotic	**o antibiótico**	oo angteebeeoteekoo
aspirin	**a aspirina**	a ashpeereena

bandage	a ligadura	a leegadoora
band-aids	os adesivos	oosh adəzeevoosh
contraceptive	o contraceptivo	oo kawngtraseteevoo
corn plaster	os adesivos para calos	oosh adəzeevoosh para kahloosh
cotton wool	a algodão	oo ahlgoodowng
cough lozenges	as pastilhas para a tosse	ash pashteellyash para a tosə
cough mixture	o xarope para a tosse	oo sharopə para a tosə
disinfectant	o desinfectante	oo dəzeengfetangtə
ear drops	os pingos para os ouvidos	oosh peenggoosh para oosh awveedoosh
gargle	gargarejar	gargarəzhahr
gauze	a gaze	a gahzə
insect repellant	o mata moscas	oo mahta mawshkash
iodine	a tintura de iodo	a teengtoora də eeawdoo
iron pills	as pastilhas de ferro	ash pashteellyash də ferroo
laxative	o laxativo	oo lashateevoo
lip salve	o batom de ceeiro	oo batawng de seeayroo
sanitary towels	os pensos higiénicos	oosh pehngsoosh eezhee-eneekoosh
sedative	o calmante	oo kahlmangtə
sleeping pills	os comprimidos para dormir	oosh kawngprəmeedoosh para doormeer
thermometer	o termómetro	oo tərmomətroo
tranquilizers	os calmantes	oosh kahlmangtəsh
vitamins	as vitaminas	ash veetameenash

TOILET ARTICLES

after-shave	o after-shave	oo after-shave
astringent	o astringente	oo ashtreengzhehngtə
bath oil	óleo de banho	oo oleeoo də banyoo
bath salts	os sais de banho	oosh sysh də banyoo
cologne	a água de colónia	a ahgooa də kooloneea
comb	o pente	oo pehngtə

cream	o creme	oo kremə
cleansing	a limpeza	a leengpehza
cuticle	a cutícula	a kooteekoola
foundation	a base	a bahzə
moisturizing	o hidratante	oo eedratangtə
deodorant	o desodorizante	oo dezodəreezangtə
emery board	a lima	a leema
eye pencil	o lápis para os olhos	oo lahpeesh para oosh ollyoosh
eye shadow	a sombra	a sawngbra
face pack	a máscara	a mahshkara
face powder	o pó de arroz	oo po də arrawsh
hairbrush	a escova	a əshkawva
hair spray	a laca	a lahka
lipstick	o batom	oo batawng
mascara	o rímel	oo reemel
nailbrush	a escova de unhas	a əshkawva də oonyash
nailfile	a lima de unhas	a leema də oonyash
nail polish	o verniz	oo vərneesh
nail polish remover	a acetona	a asətawna
nail scissors	a tesoura de unhas	a təzawra də oonyash
nappies	as fraldas	ash frahldash
nappy pins	os alfinetes de fralda	oosh ahlfeenehtəsh də frahlda
perfume	o perfume	oo pərfoomə
plastic pants	as calças de plástico	ash kahlsash də plahshteekoo
rouge	o rouge	oo rroozhə
safety pins	os alfinetes de ama	oosh ahlfeenehtəsh də ama
shampoo	o shampô	oo shangpaw
shaving brush	o pincel da barba	oo peengsel da bahrba
shaving cream	o creme de barbear	oo kremə də barbeeahr
soap	o sabonete	oo saboonehtə
sponge	a esponja	a əshpawngzha
suntan oil	o óleo de bronzear	oo oleeoo də brawngzeeahr
tissues	os lenços de papel	oosh lehngsoosh də papel

toilet paper	o papel higiénico	oo papel eezhee-eneekoo
toothbrush	a escova de dentes	a eshkawva də dehngtəsh
toothpaste	a pasta de dentes	a pahshta də dehngtəsh
tweezers	as pinças	ash peengsash

At the Photographer's

I'd like to buy a camera.	Queria comprar uma máquina fotográfica.	kəreea kawngprahr ooma mahkeena footoograhfeeka
I'd like a camera that is cheap and easy to use.	Queria uma máquina que fosse barata e fácil de utilisar.	kəreea ooma mahkeena kə fawsə barahta ee fahseel də ootəleezahr
Will you please check my camera?	Podia verificar a minha máquina, se faz favor?	poodeea vəreefeekahr a meenya mahkeena sə fahsh favawr
The film is sticking.	O filme encrava-se.	oo feelmə ehngkrahva-sə
The exposure meter is not working.	A célula foto-eléctrica não funciona.	a seloola foto-eeletreeka nowng foongseeawna
The flash does not light up.	O flash não acende.	oo flahsh nowng asehngdə
The film winder is jammed.	O carreto está encravado.	oo karrehtoo əshtah ehngkravahdoo
Can you do it soon?	Pode fazer rápidamente?	podə fazehr rahpeedamehngtə
Will you please process this film?	Podia mandar revelar este filme?	podeea mangdahr rrəvəlahr ehshtə feelmə
I would like prints with a matt finish/a glossy finish.	Queria as fotografias em baço/as fotografias brilhantes.	kəreea ash footoografeeash ayng bahsoo/ash footoografeeash breellyangtəsh

I want a black and white film/a colour film/a Polaroid film.	**Quero um filme a preto e branco/um filme a cores/um filme Polaroid.**	

keroo oong feelmə a prehtoo ee brangkoo/oong feelmə a kawrəsh/oong feelmə polaroid

Is this film for use in daylight or artificial light?	**Este filme é para ser utilisado à luz natural ou eléctrica?**

ehshtə feelmə e para sehr ootəleezahdoo ah loosh natoorahl aw eeletreeka

I should like a 35-mm film.	**Queria un filme de trinta e cinco milímetros.**

kəreea oong feelmə de treengta e seengkoo meeleemətroosh

I need a light meter.	**Preciso de um fotómetro.**

prəseezoo də oong footomətroo

How much is an electronic flash?	**Quanto é que custa um flash electrónico?**

kooangtoo e kə kooshta oong flahsh eeletroneeko

Vocabulary

120 film	**filme de cento e vinte**	feelmə de sehngtoo ee veengtə
127 film	**filme de cento e vinte sete**	feelmə de sehngtoo ee veengtə setə
135 film	**filme de cento e trinta e cinco**	feelmə de sehngtoo ee treengta ee seengkoo
620 film	**filme de seiscentos e vinte**	feelmə de sayshsehngtoosh ee veengtə
24 exposures	**vinte e quatro fotografias**	veengtə ee kooahtroo footoografeeash
36 exposures	**trinta e seis fotografias**	treengta ee saysh footoografeeash
camera case	**o estojo**	oo eeshtawzhoo

cinefilm 8mm/16mm	**um cinefilme de oito milímetros/de dezasseis milímetros**	oong seenefeelmə də oytoo meeleemətroosh/də dezasaysh meeleemətroosh
colour slides	**os diapositivos a cores**	oosh deeapoozeeteevoosh a kawrəsh
(to) develop	**revelar**	rrəvəlahr
fast film	**um filme de muita sensibilidade**	oong feelmə də mooeengta sehngsəbəleedahdə
fine-grain film	**um filme com grão muito fino**	oong feelmə kawng growng mooeengtoo feenoo
flash bulb	**a lâmpada de flash**	a langpada de flahsh
lens	**a lente**	a lehngtə
lens cap	**a tampa para a lente**	a tangpa para a lehngtə
long-focus lens	**a lente de focagem**	a lehngtə de fookahzhayng
photograph	**a fotografia**	a footoografeea
photographer	**o fotógrafo**	o footografoo
(to) print	**imprimir**	eengprəmeer
range finder	**o telémetro**	oo telemetroo
red filter	**o filtro vermelho**	oo feeltroo vermellyoo
reflex camera	**o sistema reflectivo**	oo seeshtehma refleteevoo
shutter	**o obturador**	oo obtooradawr
ultra-violet filter	**o filtro ultra violeta**	oo feeltroo ooltra veeoolehta
wide-angle lens	**a grande angular**	a grangdə anggoolahr
yellow filter	**o filtro amarelo**	oo feeltroo amareloo

Bookshop/Stationer's

Where can I find the books on art/on history/on politics/on sport?	**Onde é que estão os livros de arte/de história/de política/de desporto?** awngde e kə əshtowng oosh leevroosh də ahrtə/də əshtoreea/də pooleeteeka/də dəshpawrtoo
Where can I find the guide books?	**Onde estão os guias turísticos?** awngdə əshtowng oosh geeash tooreeshteekoosh
Have you any English newspapers?	**Tem jornais ingleses?** tehng zhoornysh eengglehzəsh
Have you any English paperbacks?	**Tem livros de bolso ingleses?** tehng leevroosh də bawlsoo eengglehzəsh?
Can you recommend an easy book to read in Portuguese?	**Pode-me recomendar um livro português que seja fácil de se ler?** podə-mə rrəkoomehngdahr oong leevroo poortoogehsh kə sehzha fahseel də sə lehr
Do you sell second-hand books?	**Vendem livros em segunda mão?** vehngdayng leevroosh ayng səgoongda mowng
I want a map of the area.	**Queria um mapa da região.** kəreea oong mahpa da rrəzheeowng
The scale of this map is too small.	**A escala deste mapa é pequena demais.** a əshkahla dehshtə mahpa e pəkehna dəmysh
Have you got refills for this ballpoint pen?	**Tem cargas para esta esferográfica?** tehng kahrgash para eshta eshferograhfeeka
Can you please deliver the English newspaper every morning?	**Podia mandar entregar o jornal inglês todas as manhãs?** poodeea mangdahr ehngtrəgahr oo zhoornahl eengglehsh tawdash ash manyash

VOCABULARY

address book	o livro de moradas [endereços]	oo leevroo də moorahdash [ehngderehsoos]
box of crayons	a caixa de lápis de côr	a kysha də lahpeesh də kawr
carbon paper	o papel químico	oo papel keemeekoo
cellophane	o celofane	oo selofanə
drawing pins	os pionés	oosh peeonesh
envelopes	os envelopes	oosh ehngvəlopəsh
exercise book	o caderno	oo kadernoo
fountain pen	a caneta de tinta permanente	a kanehta de teengta pərmanehngtə
glue	a cola	a kola
greaseproof paper	o papel vegetal	oo papel vəzhətahl
ink	a tinta	a teengta
label	a etiqueta	a eeteekehta
magazines	as revistas	ash rrəveeshtash
notebook	o bloco	oo blokoo
notepaper	o papel de carta	oo papel də kahrta
paste	a cola branca	a kola brangka
pen	a caneta	a kanehta
pencil	o lápis	oo lahpeesh
pencil sharpener	o apara-lápis	oo apahra-lahpeesh
playing cards	as cartas de jogar	ash kahrtash de zhoogahr
postcards	os postais	oosh pooshtysh
rubber	a borracha	a boorrahsha
ruler	a régua	a rregooa
silver foil	o papel de prata	oo papel də prahta
sketchpad	o bloco de desenho	oo blokoo də dəsehnyoo
tissue paper	o papel de seda	oo papel də sehda
typewriter ribbon	a fita para a máquina	a feeta para a mahkeena
typing paper	o papél de máquina	oo papel də mahkeena
writing pad	o bloco	oo blokoo

Buying Souvenirs

Are all these things made in Portugal?	**Isto tudo foi fabricado em Portugal?** eeshtoo toodoo foy fabreekahdoo ayng poortoogahl
This is a nice straw hat.	**Este chapéu de palha é bonito.** ehshtə shapeoo də pahllya e booneetoo
I like this bag.	**Gosto desta carteira.** goshtoo deshta kartayra
Have you any costume jewellery?	**Tem joias de fantasia?** tehng zhoeeash də fangtazeea
I'm looking for bracelet charms.	**Estou à procura de penduricalhos para pendurar numa pulseira.** əshtaw ah prokoora də pehngdooreekahllyoosh para pehngdoorahr nooma poolsayra
I'd like to try on that ring.	**Queria experimentar esse anel.** kəreea əshpəreemehngtahr ehsə anel
What is this bracelet made of?	**Esta pulseira é feita de quê?** eshta poolsayra e fayta də keh
I collect copperware.	**Faço colecção de artigos de cobre.** fahsoo koolesowng də arteegoosh də kobrə
Have you any pots?	**Tem vasos?** tehng vazoosh
I'd like some local pottery.	**Queria comprar artigos de cerâmica regional.** kereea kawngprahr arteegoosh de sərameeka rrezheeoonahl
Can you pack this carefully?	**Pode embrulhar isto bem?** podə ehngbroollyar eeshtoo bayng
Do you despatch things abroad?	**Mandam coisas para o estrangeiro?** mangdang koyzash para oo əshtrangzhayroo
I'm just looking around.	**Estou só a ver.** eshtaw so a vehr

I will come back later.	**Volto mais tarde.**	
	voltoo mysh **tahrd**ə	
Can I leave a deposit on it and return tomorrow?	**Posso deixar um depósito e voltar amanhã?**	
	posoo day**shahr** oong də**pozee**too ee vol**tahr** ahman**yang**	
Do you take foreign cheques with a Eurocard?	**Aceitam cheques estrangeiros com um cartão Eurocheque?**	
	asay**tang** she**kəsh** əshtrang**zhay**roosh kawng oong kar**towng** ehooro**shek**ə	

VOCABULARY

beads	**o colar**	oo koo**lahr**
brooch	**o broche**	oo **brosh**ə
chain	**o fio**	oo **fee**oo
cigarette lighter	**o isqueiro**	oo eesh**kay**roo
clock	**o relógio**	oo rrə**lozhee**oo
costumes	**os fatos**	oosh **fah**toosh
cuff links	**os botões de punho**	oosh boo**toyngsh** də **poon**yoo
doll	**a boneca**	a **boon**eka
earrings	**os brincos**	oosh **breeng**koosh
jewel box	**o cofre de jóias**	oo **kofr**ə də **zho**eeash
leatherwork	**o couro trabalhado**	oo **kaw**roo traba**llyah**doo
music box	**a caixa musical**	a **kysh**a moozee**kahl**
necklace	**o colar**	oo koo**lahr**
pewterware	**os artigos de estanho**	oosh ar**tee**goosh də əsh**tan**yoo
rosary	**o terço**	oo **tehr**soo
silverware	**as pratas**	ash **prah**tash
souvenir	**a lembrança**	a lehng**brang**sa
watchstrap	**a correia de relógio**	a koo**rray**a də rrə**lozhee**oo
wristwatch	**o relógio de pulso**	oo rrə**lozhee**oo də **pool**soo

Entertainment

Out for the Evening

Nightclubs

Can you recommend
Pode-me recomendar
podə-mə rrəkoomehngdahr

a nightclub with a good show?
uma boîte com um bom espectaculo?
ooma booahte kawng oong bawng əshpetahkooloo

a place with dancing and cabaret?
um sítio onde se possa dançar e que tenha cabaret?
oong seeteeoo awngdə sə posa dangsahr ee kə tehnya kahbahre

a disco?
uma discoteca?
ooma deeshkooteka

an open-air dance?
um baile ao ar livre?
oong bylə aoo ahr leevrə

Is there an entrance fee?
Paga-se à entrada?
pahga-sə ah ehngtrahda

Does it include drinks?
Inclui as bebidas?
eengklooee ash bəbeedash

What is the cost of drinks?
Quanto é que custam as bebidas?
kooangtoo e kə kooshtang ash bəbeedash

At what time does the show start?
A que horas é que começa o espectáculo?
a kə orash e kə koomesa oo əshpetahkooloo

Is there a different price for drinks at the bar?
Existe uma differença de preço nas bebidas compradas no bar?
eezeeshtə ooma deefərehngsa də prehsoosh nash bəbeedash kawngprahdash noo bahr

I do not want a photograph.	**Não quero fotografias.**	nowng keroo footoografeeash
Would you like to dance?	**Quer dançar?**	ker dangsahr

Theatre/Opera

Is there a ticket agency near?	**Há uma agência de bilhetes aqui perto?**	ah ooma azhehngseea də bəllyehtəsh akee pertoo
How can I get a ticket?	**Como é que arranjo bilhete?**	kawmoo e kə arrangzhoo bəllyehtə
Are there any last-minute returns?	**Haverá alguma desistência à última hora?**	avərah ahlgooma dəzeeshtehngseea ah oolteema ora
Do we have to wear evening dress?	**Tem que se ir de smoking?**	tehng kə sə eer də smokeeng
I'd like a programme.	**Queria um programa.**	kəreea oong proograma
What is the name of the prima donna?	**Como se chama a prima donna?**	kawmoo sə shama a preema dona?
Who is the leading actor/actress?	**Quem é o actor principal/a actriz principal?**	kayng e oo ahtawr preengseepahl/a ahtreesh preengseepahl

contralto	**a contralto**	a kawngtrahltoo
encore	**bis**	beezh
opera	**a ópera**	a opera
orchestra	**a orquestra**	a orkeshtra
playwright	**o dramaturgo**	oo dramatoorgoo
scenery	**os cenários**	oosh sənahreeoosh
soprano	**a soprano**	a soopranoo
stage	**o palco**	oo pahlkoo
tenor	**o tenor**	oo tenawr
theatre	**o teatro**	oo teeahtroo

Cinema

What is on at the cinema?

O que é que vai no cinema?
oo kə e kə vy noo seenehma?

Have you got a guide to what's on?

Tem uma lista dos espectáculos?
tehng ooma leeshta doosh əshpetahkooloosh

Two stalls/circle seats, please.

Dois bilhetes para a plateia/para o primeiro balcão, por favor.
doysh bəllyehtəsh para a plataya/para oo preemayroo bahlkowng, poor favawr

Will we have to queue for long?

Vamos ter que fazer bicha [fila] durante muito tempo?
vamoosh tehr kə fazehr beesha [feela] doorangtə mooeengtoo tehngpoo

I want a seat near the front/at the back/in the middle.

Quero um lugar à frente/atrás/no centro.
keroo oong loogahr/ah frehngtə/atrahsh/noo sehngtroo

rather sit over

Preferia sentar-me ali.
prəfəreea sehngtahr-mə alee

dropped

Deixei cair uma coisa.
dayshay kaeer ooma koyza

e cream

Vendem gelados lá dentro?
vehngdayng zhəlahdoosh lah dehngtroo

At what time does the main film start?

A que horas é que começa o filme principal?
a kə orash e kə koomesa oo feelmə preengseepahl

Will you please move over to the right/left.

Pode-se chegar à direita/à esquerda se faz favor.
podə-sə shəgahr ah deerayta/ah əshkehrda sə fahsh favawr

Please will you remove your hat.

Podia tirar o chapéu se faz favor.
poodeea teerahr oo shapeoo sə fahsh favawr

VOCABULARY

actor	o actor	oo ahtawr
actress	a actriz	a ahtreesh
director	o realizador	oo reealeezadawr
dubbing	a dobragem	a doobrahzhayng
film	o filme	oo feelmə
interval	o intervalo	oo eengtərvahloo
producer	o produtor	oo proodootawr
projector	o projector	oo proozhetawr
screen	o écran	oo ekrang
seat	o lugar	oo loogahr
sound	o som	oo sawng
star	a estrela	a əshtrehla

Concert Hall

I want a seat from which I can see the pianist's hands.

Queria um lugar de onde se possa ver as mãos do pianista.
kəreea oong loogahr dawngdə sə posa vehr ash mowngsh doo peeaneeshta

Can I buy the score?

Posso comprar a partitura?
posoo kawngprahr a parteetoora

Who is conducting tonight?

Quem é o maestro hoje?
kayng e oo maeshtroo awzhə

| Who is the soloist? | **Quem é o solista?** |
| | kayng e oo sooleeshta. |

VOCABULARY

bassoon	o fagote	oo fagotə
brass	os metais	oosh mətysh
cello	o violoncelo	oo veeoolawngseloo
choir	o coro	oo kawroo
clarinet	o clarinete	oo klareenehte
conductor	o maestro	oo maeshtroo
cymbal	o címbalo	oo seengbaloo
double bass	o contrabaixo	oo kawngtrabyshoo
drum	o tambor	oo tangbawr
flute	a flauta	a flowta
French horn	o corne inglês	oo kornə eengglehsh
harp	a harpa	a ahrpa
oboe	o oboé	oo obooe
percussion	a percussão	a pərkoosowng
saxophone	o saxofone	oo sahksofone
strings	as cordas	ash kordash
timpani	os tímbales	oosh teengbaləsh
trombone	o trombone	oo trawngbonə
trumpet	o trompete	oo trawngpehtə
violin	o violino	oo veeooleenoo
wind instrument	o instrumento de sopro	oo eengshtroomehngtoo də sawproo

Casino

What games are played here?	**O que é que se joga aqui?**
	oo kə e kə sə zhoga akee
What is the minimum ke in this room?	**Qual é a aposta mínima aqui?**
	kooahl e a aposhta meeneema akee
uy some chips?	**Posso comprar fichas?**
	posoo kawngprahr feeshash

I should like 200 escudos' worth.	**Queria comprar duzentos escudos de fichas.**	kəreea kawngprahr doozhehngtoosh əshkoodoosh də feeshash
Excuse me, those are my chips.	**Desculpe, essas são as minhas fichas.**	dəshkoolpə esash sowng ash meenyash feeshash
Where can I cash my chips?	**Aonde é que posso trocar as minhas fichas?**	aawngde e kə posoo trokahr ash meenyash feeshash
I'm bust.	**Arrebentei.**	arrəbehngtay
I'll take another card.	**Quero outra carta.**	keroo awtra kahrta
No more.	**Chega.**	shehga
Pass me the dice, please.	**Passe-me os dados, se faz favor.**	pahsə-mə oosh dahdoosh poor favawr

VOCABULARY

ace	**o ás**	oo ahsh
banker	**a banca**	a bangka
bet	**a aposta**	a aposhta
cards	**as cartas**	ash kahrtash
chemin de fer	**chemin de fer**	shəmen də ferr
clubs	**paus**	powsh
craps	**dados**	dahdoosh
croupier	**o croupier**	oo kroopee-ehr
diamonds	**ouros**	awroosh
evens	**pares**	pahrəsh
hearts	**copas**	kopash
jack	**o valete**	oo valetə
joker	**o jóquer**	oo zhokər
king	**o rei**	oo rray
poker	**o póker**	oo pokər
pontoon	**vinte e um**	veengtə ee oom

queen	**a rainha**	a rraeenya
shoe	**a pá**	a pah
spades	**espadas**	əshpahdash

Out for the Day

On the Beach

| Is the beach clean? | **É limpa a praia?** |
| | e leengpa a prya |

How much does it cost to hire	**Quanto é que custa alugar**
	kooangtoo e kə kooshta aloogahr
a cabin?	**uma barraca?**
	ooma barrahka
a deckchair?	**uma cadeira de lona?**
	ooma kadayra də lawna
an air mattress?	**um colchão?**
	oong kolshowng
a sun umbrella?	**um guarda-sol?**
	oong gooahrda-sol
per day?	**por dia?**
	poor deea
per week?	**poor semana?**
	poor səmana

| Can I leave valuables in the cabin? | **Posso deixar artigos de valor na barraca?** |
| | posoo dayshahr arteegoosh də valawr na barrahka |

| Is the ticket valid all day? | **A senha é válida durante o dia inteiro?** |
| | a senya e vahleeda doorangtə oo deea eengtayroo |

| Does the beach slope steeply? | **Há um desnivelamento súbito nesta praia?** |
| | ah oong dəshneevəlamehngtoo soobeetoo neshta prya |

| Is it safe for swimming? | **Pode-se nadar?** |
| | podə-sə nadahr |

Are there any currents?	**Há correntes perigosas?** ah koorrehngtəsh pəreegozash
Is it safe to dive off the rocks?	**É perigoso mergulhar das rochas?** e pəreegawzoo mərgoollyahr dash roshash
Where are the showers?	**Onde são os chuveiros?** awngdə sowng oosh shoovayroosh
Have you any tar remover?	**Tem um produto que tire o alcatrão?** tehng oong proodootoo kə teerə oo ahlkatrowng
Can I hire a swimsuit/trunks?	**Posso alugar um fato de banho [um maiô]/calções?** posoo aloogahr oong fahtoo də banyoo [oong maeeaw]/kahlsoyngsh
I've cut my foot. Have you any elastoplast?	**Cortei o pé. Tem adesivos?** koortay oo pe. tehng adəzeevoosh
Is there a lost property office?	**Há um escritório de perdidos e achados?** ah oong əshkreetoreeoo də pərdeedoosh ee ashahdoosh
Is there a children's beach club?	**Há um clube de praia para crianças?** ah oong kloobə də prya para kreeangsash
At what time are the keep fit classes?	**A que horas são as aulas de ginástica?** a kə orash sowng ash owlash də zheenahshteeka
Is there water ski tuition available?	**Dão lições de esqui aquático?** downg leesoyngsh də əskee akooahteekoo
Does it matter if I can't swim?	**Faz diferença eu não saber nadar?** fahsh deefərehngsa ehoo nowng sabehr nadahr
Where is the nearest beach shop?	**Onde é a loja mais próxima que vende equipamento de praia?** awngdə e a lozha mysh proseema kə vehngdə eekeepamehngtoo de prya
Have you got a life jacket?	**Tem um colete de salvação?** tehng oong koolehtə də sahlvasowng
Is this a good place for skin diving?	**Este sitio é bom para a pesca submarina?** ehshtə seeteeoo e bawng para a peshka soobmareena

Where can I hire diving equipment?	**Aonde é que posso alugar equipamento de mergulho?**	
	aawngde e kə posoo aloogahr eekeepamehngtoo də mergoollyoo	
Help! I'm in trouble.	**Socorro! Estou aflito.**	
	sookawrroo! eshtaw afleetoo	

VOCABULARY

aqualung	**a garrafa de oxigenio**	a garrahfa də okseezheneeoo
beach ball	**a bola**	a bola
dinghy	**o barco a vela**	oo bahrkoo ah vela
flippers	**as barbatanas**	ash barbatanash
goggles	**os óculos de natação**	oosh okooloosh də natasowng
harpoon gun	**o arpão**	oo arpowng
high tide	**a maré alta**	a mare ahlta
lilo	**o colchão de borracha**	oo kolshowng də boorrahsha
low tide	**a maré baixa**	a mare bysha
net	**a rede**	a rrehdə
pedalo	**a gaivota**	a gyvota
pines	**os pinheiros**	oosh peenyayroosh
promenade	**o passeio**	oo pasayoo
raft	**a jangada**	a zhanggahda
rocks	**as rochas**	ash rroshash
rowing boat	**o barco a remos**	oo bahrkoo a rremoosh
sand	**a areia**	a araya
sandals	**as sandálias**	ash sangdahleeash
sea	**o mar**	oo mahr
seaweed	**as algas**	ash ahlgash
shells	**as conchas**	ash kawngshash
shingle	**as pedras**	ash pedrash
snorkel	**o tubo de respiracão**	oo tooboo də rreshpeerasowng

sun oil	óleo de bronzear	oo oleeoo də brawngzeeahr
surf	o surf	oo surf
surf board	a tábua de surf	a tahbooa də surf
underwater	debaixo de água	dəbyshoo də ahgooa
waterski instructor	o instructor de esqui aquático	oo eengshtrootawr də əskee akooahteekoo
wetsuit	o fato de mergulho	oo fahtoo de mergoollyoo
yacht	o iate	oo eeahtə

Sightseeing

Where can I get a good guide book?
Aonde é que posso comprar um bom guia turístico?
aawngde e kə posoo kawng**prahr** oong bawng geea tooreeshteekoo

Is there an excursion round the city?
Há uma excursão pela cidade?
ah ooma əshkoor**sowng** pehla seedahdə

Is it a conducted party?
A excursão tem guia?
a əshkoor**sowng** tehng geea

Am I allowed to go round alone?
Posso passear sózinho(a)?
posoo paseeahr sozeenyoo(a)

Where do I find an official guide?
Aonde é que está o guia oficial?
aawngde e kə əshtah oo geea ofeeseeahl

Does the whole-day excursion include lunch?
A excursão do dia inteiro inclui almoço?
a əshkoor**sowng** doo **deea** eengtayroo eengk**looee** ahlmawsoo

Are the entrance fees extra?
As entradas custam extra?
ash ehngtrahdash **koosh**tang ay**sh**tra

Should I tip the guide/the driver?
Devo dar gorgeta ao guia/ao motorista?
dehvoo dahr goorzhehta ow geea/ow mootoo**reesh**ta

I'd like to stay here longer.
Queria ficar aqui mais tempo.
kəreea feekahr akee mysh tehngpoo

I'll meet the party later.

Encontro-me com o grupo mais tarde.
ehngkawngtroo-mə kawng oo groopoo mysh tahrdə

Where will you be?

Aonde é que vocês vão estar?
aawngde e kə vosehsh vowng əshtahr

Will you please write it down?

Podia escrever isso se faz favor?
poodeea əshkrevehr eesoo sə fahsh favawr

Can I hire an audioguide?

Posso alugar um audio-guia?
posoo aloogahr oong owdeeoo-geea

In Churches

Do ladies have to cover their heads?

As senhoras têm que cobrir a cabeça?
ash senyawrash tayehng kə koobreer a kabehsa

Is it all right to enter like this?

Pode-se entrar assim vestido?
podə-sə ehngtrahr aseeng vəshteedoo

How old is this church?

Quantos anos tem esta igreja?
kooangtoosh anoosh tehng eshta eegrayzha

Who founded it?

Quem é que a construiu?
kayng e kə a kawngshtrooeeoo

Are the stained glass windows original?

Os vitrais são autênticos?
oosh veetrysh sowng owtehngteekoosh

Can one illuminate the fresco?

Pode-se iluminar este mural?
podə-sə eeloomeenahr ehshtə moorahl

Is one allowed to go up to the bell tower?

Pode-se subir ao campanário?
podə-sə soobeer ow kangpanahreeoo

Is there a book about the church?

Há algum livro sobre esta igreja?
ah ahlgoong leevroo sawbrə eshta eegrayzha

May I leave a small contribution?

Posso contribuir com qualquer coisa?
posoo kawngtreebooeer kawng kooahlker koyza

Vocabulary

abbey	a abadia	a abadeea
aisles	as alas	ash ahlash
altar	o altar	oo ahltahr
arch	o arco	oo ahrkoo
basilica	a basílica	a bazeeleeka
candle	a vela	a vela
cathedral	a catedral	a katedrahl
chapel	a capela	a kapela
choir	o côro	oo kawroo
cloister	o claustro	oo klowshtroo
column	a coluna	a kooloona
convent	o convento	oo kawngvehngtoo
crucifix	o crucifixo	oo kroosəfeeksoo
crypt	a cripta	a kreepta
font	a pia baptismal	a peea bahteeshmahl
fresco	o mural/o fresco	oo moorahl/oo frehshkoo
monastery	o mosteiro	oo mooshtayroo
nave	a nave	a nahvə
rood screen	o guarda-vento	oo gooahrda- vehngtoo
sculpture	a escultura	a əshkooltoora
shrine	o oratório	oo oratoreeo
west front	a fachada ocidental	a fashahda oseedehngtahl

Signs

Fechado para obras   Closed for repairs
Fechado para restauração   Closed for restoration
Proibido tirar fotografias   No photographs

Art Galleries and Museums

Have you a catalogue/ an illustrated catalogue?   **Tem un catálogo/um catálogo ilustrado?**
tehng oong katahloogoo/oong katahloogoo eelooshtrahdoo

Are there any plaster casts?	**Vendem moldes de gesso?**	vehngdayng moldəsh də zhehsoo
Do you sell transparencies?	**Vendem diapositivos (slides)?**	vehngdayng deeapoozeeteevoosh (slides)
Am I allowed to take photographs?	**Posso tirar fotografias?**	posoo teerahr fotoografeeash
May I use my tripod?	**Posso utilisar o meu tripé?**	posoo ootəleezahr o mehoo treepe
Is the gallery/museum open every day?	**A galeria/o museu está aberta(to) todos os dias?**	a galəreea/oo moozehoo əshtah aberta(too) tawdoosh oosh deeash
Is the gallery open on Sundays?	**A galeria está aberta ao Domingo?**	a galəreea əshtah aberta ow doomeenggoo
Is it free?	**É grátis?**	e grahteesh
Where can I find the Dutch School?	**Onde estão os quadros da escola holandesa?**	awngde əshtowng oosh kooahdroosh da əshkola olangdehza?
Do you make photocopies?	**Fazem fotocópias?**	fahzayng fotokopeeash
Where can we buy postcards?	**Aonde é que se pode comprar postais?**	awngde e kə sə podə kawngprahr pooshtysh
Where is the library?	**Onde é a biblioteca?**	awngde e a beebleeooteka

VOCABULARY

antique books	**os livros antigos**	oosh leevroosh angteegoosh
bas relief	**o baixo relevo**	oo bysho relehvoo
china	**a porcelana**	a poorsəlana
costumes	**os trajes**	oosh trahzhes

drawing	o desenho	oo dəzenyoo
engraving	a gravura	a gravoora
etching	a gravura	a gravoora
frame	a moldura	a moldoora
furniture	a mobília	a moobeeleea
jewellery	as jóias	ash zhoeeash
lithograph	a litografia	a leetoografeea
miniature	a miniatura	a meeneeatoora
porcelain	a porcelana	a poorsəlana
pottery	a cerâmica	a sərameeka
silverware	as pratas	ash prahtash

Historical Sights

Will there be far to walk?	**Tem que se andar muito?** tehng kə sə angdahr mooeengtoo
Can I wait here till you return?	**Posso esperar aqui até vocês voltarem?** posoo əshperahr akee ate vosehsh voltahrayng
Is there a souvenir stall?	**Vendem aqui lembranças?** vehngdayng akee lehngbrangsash
Where can we get a cold drink?	**Onde é que podemos comprar uma bebida fresca?** awngde e kə poodehmoosh kawngprahr ooma bəbeeda frehshka
Is there a plan of the grounds?	**Há um plano dos jardins?** ah oong planoo doosh zhardeengsh
I would like to walk round the gardens.	**Queria dar um passeio pelos jardins.** kəreea dahr oong pasayoo pehloosh zhardeengsh

VOCABULARY

| amphitheatre | o anfiteatro/o circo | oo angfeeteeahtroo/oo seerkoo |
| aqueduct | o aqueducto | oo akədootoo |

arena	**a arena**	a arehna
armour	**a armadura**	a ahrmadoora
battlements	**as ameias**	ash amayash
cannon	**o canhão**	oo kanyowng
castle	**o castelo**	oo kashteloo
catacombs	**as catacombas**	ash katakawngbash
courtyard	**o pátio**	oo pahteeoo
crossbow	**a besta**	a behshta
fort	**a fortaleza**	a foortalehza
fortifications	**as fortificações**	ash foortəfeekasoyngsh
forum	**o foro**	oo fawroo
fountain	**a fonte**	a fawngtə
gate	**o portão**	oo poortowng
palace	**o palácio**	oo palahseeoo
pediment	**o frontão**	oo frawngtowng
portcullis	**a ponte levadiça**	a pawngtə ləvadeesa
temple	**o templo**	oo tehngploo
tower	**a torre**	a tawrrə
viaduct	**o viaducto**	oo veeadootoo
wall	**a parede**	a parehdə

Gardens

Are these gardens open to the public?	**Estes jardins estão abertos ao público?** ehshtəsh zhardeengsh əshtowng abertoosh ow poobleekoo
Can we walk where we like?	**Podemos passear por onde nos apetecer?** poodehmoosh passeeahr poor awngdə noosh apətəsehr
How long will it take to walk around?	**Quanto tempo é que demora a dar a volta a pé?** kooangtoo tehngpoo e kə dəmora a dahr a volta a pe
At what time do you close?	**A que horas é que fecham?** a kə orash e kə fayshang
Is there a plan of the gardens?	**Há um plano dos jardins?** ah oong planoo doosh zhardeengsh

Where is the greenhouse/tropical plant house?	**Aonde é que é a estufa/as plantas tropicais?** aawngde e kə e a əshtoofa/ash plangtash troopeekysh
May we sit on the grass?	**Podemo-nos sentar na relva?** poodehmoo-noosh sehngtahr na rrelva
What is the name of that plant/flower?	**Como é que se chama essa planta/essa flor?** kawmoo e kə sə shama esa plangta/esa flawr
Is there a lake?	**Há um lago?** ah oong lahgoo
Who designed these gardens?	**Quem é que desenhou estes jardins?** kayng e kə dəsənyaw ehshtəsh zhardeengsh

VOCABULARY

ash	o freixo	oo frayshoo
beech	a faia	a fya
birch	o vidoeiro	oo veedooayroo
bougainvillea	a bouganvília	a booganveeleea
carnation	o cravo	oo krahvoo
cherry tree	a cerejeira	a sərəzhayra
chestnut	o castanheiro	oo kashtanyayroo
chrysanthemum	o crisântemo	oo kreezangtəmoo
clematis	o clematite	oo kləmateetə
conifer	a conífera	a kooneefəra
daffodil	o narciso	oo nahrseezoo
dahlia	a dália	a dahleea
daisy	a margarida	a margareeda
deciduous trees	as árvores caducas	ash ahrvoorəsh kadookash
elm	o olmo	oo awlmoo
evergreen	a árvore de folha perene	a ahrvoore de fawllya pərene
fir	o abeto	oo abehtoo
geranium	o gerânio	oo gəraneeoo
herbaceous border	o canteiro herbáceo	oo kangtayroo eerbahseeoo

ivy	a hera	a era
lily	o lírio	oo leereeoo
moss	o musgo	oo moozhgoo
nasturtium	o nastúrcio	oo nashtoorseeoo
oak	o carvalho	oo karvahllyoo
palm tree	a palmeira	a pahlmayra
pear tree	a pereira	a pərayra
pine	o pinheiro	oo peenyayroo
plane	o plátano	oo plahtanoo
poplar	o choupo	oo shawpoo
rose	a rosa	a roza
tulip	a túlipa	a tooleepa
violet	a violeta	a veeoolehta
wisteria	a glicínia	a gleeseeneea

The Zoo

The children would like to visit the zoo.	As crianças gostariam de ir ao jardim zoologico. ash kreeangsash gooshtareeang də eer ow zhardeeng zoolozheekoo
Is it open every day?	Está aberto o dia inteiro? əshtah abertoo oo deea eengtayroo
Is there a nature reserve?	Há uma reserva de animais? ah ooma rreserva də aneemysh
Can one drive through it?	Pode-se atravessar de carro? podə-sə atravesahr də kahrroo
Where can we park the car?	Aonde é que se estaciona o carro? aawngde e kə sə əshtaseeawna oo kahrroo
Can we feed the animals?	Podemos dar de comer aos animais? poodehmoosh dahr də koomehr owsh aneemysh
Where can one buy animal food?	Aonde é que se compra comida para animais? aawngde e kə sə kawngpra koomeeda para aneemysh
When is feeding time?	A que horas é que dão de comer aos animais? a kə orash e kə downg də koomehr owsh aneemysh

| Is there an insect house? | **Há uma secção de insectos?**
 ah ooma seksowng də eengsetoosh |
| Is there a children's zoo? | **Há um jardim zoológico para crianças?**
 ah oong zhardeeng zoolozheekoo para kreeangsash |

VOCABULARY

ant	**a formiga**	a foormeega
antelope	**o antílope**	oo angteeloopə
aquarium	**o aquário**	oo akooahreeoo
baboon	**o macaco**	oo makahkoo
bat	**o mocho**	oo mawshoo
bird	**o pássaro**	oo pahsaroo
bison	**o bisonte**	oo beezawngtə
cat	**o gato**	oo gahtoo
crocodile	**o crocodilo**	oo krookoodeeloo
dog	**o cão [o cachorro]**	oo kowng [oo kashawrroo]
frog	**a rã**	a rrang
giraffe	**a girafa**	a zheerahfa
hippopotamus	**o hipopótamo**	oo eepopotamoo
horse	**o cavalo**	oo kavahloo
hyena	**a hiena**	a ee-ehna
leopard	**o leopardo**	oo leeopahrdoo
lion	**o leão**	oo leeowng
monkey	**o macaco**	oo makahkoo
parrot	**o papagaio**	oo papagyoo
rhinoceros	**o rinoceronte**	oo rreenosərawngtə
seal	**a foca**	a foka
snake	**a cobra**	a kobra
tiger	**o tigre**	oo teegrə
turtle	**a tartaruga**	a tartarooga
zebra	**a zebra**	a zehbra

Sport

The two chief spectator sports in Portugal are football and the bullfight. The Portuguese bullfight is quite different from the Spanish one and consists of a phase where a horseman tires the bull out and places small darts or **farpas** on it and a final phase where eight men try to bring the bull to a standstill without the aid of weapons of any kind. The animal is not killed in the bullring. Other sports available at holiday resorts are water sports, golf, tennis and fishing, especially deep-sea fishing.

The Bullfight

I would like to go to a bullfight.	**Gostava de ir a uma tourada.** gooshtahva də eer a ooma tawrahda
Where is the arena?	**Onde é a praça de touros?** awngde e a prahsa də tawroosh
When is the next bullfight?	**Quando é próxima tourada?** kooangdoo e a proseema tawrahda
I want a ringside seat.	**Quero um lugar nas primeiras filas.** keroo oong loogahr nash preemayrash feelash
I want a seat in the shade/in the sun.	**Quero um lugar à sombra/ao sol.** keroo oong loogahr ah sawngbra/ow sol
Can I hire a cushion?	**Posso alugar uma almofada?** posoo aloogahr ooma ahlmoofahda
Is there a programme?	**Vendem programas?** vehngdayng proogramash
No thank you, I do not want to buy souvenirs.	**Não obrigado(a), não quero comprar nada.** nowng obreegahdoo(a), nowng keroo kawngprahr nahda.

Vocabulary

bull	**o touro**	oo tawroo
bullfighter	**o toureiro**	oo tawrayroo
bullring	**a praça de touros/a arena**	a prahsa de tawroosh/a arehna
cloak	**a capa**	a kahpa
dart	**a bandarilha**	a bangdareellya
gate	**a porta**	a porta
horns	**os chifres**	oosh sheefrəsh
horseman	**o cavaleiro**	oo kavalayroo
sand	**a areia**	a araya

Football

Where is the stadium?	**Onde é o estádio?**	awngde e oo əshtahdeeoo
How does one get there?	**Como é que se vai para lá?**	kawmoo e kə sə vy para lah
Should I book tickets?	**É preciso marcar bilhetes?**	e prəseezoo markahr beellyehtəsh
Will it be very crowded?	**Vai estar cheio?**	vy əshtahr shayoo
Who is playing?	**Que equipas é que jogam?**	kə eekeepash e kə zhogang
Is there a local team?	**Há uma equipa local?**	ah ooma eekeepa lookahl
I want	**Quero**	keroo
a ticket for the main stand.	**um bilhete para a bancada principal.**	oong bəllyehtə para a bangkahda preengseepahl
a place under cover.	**um lugar coberto.**	oong loogahr koobertoo

I want	**Quero**
	keroo
a place in the open.	**um lugar ao ar livre.**
	oong loogahr ow ahr leevrə
May I have a programme?	**Dava-me um programa?**
	dahva-mə oong proograma
What is the score?	**Qual e o resultado?**
	kooahl e oo rrəzooltahdoo

VOCABULARY

area	**a área**	a ahreea
attack	**ataque**	atahkə
centre half	**o médio**	oo medeeoo
defence	**a defesa**	a defehza
fans	**os fans**	oosh fangsh
foul	**a falta**	a fahlta
forwards	**os avançados**	oosh avangsahdoosh
goal	**o golo**	oo gawloo
goalkeeper	**o guarda-redes**	oo gooahrda rrehdəsh
goal posts	**os postes da baliza**	oosh poshtəsh da baleeza
halfway line	**a linha de meio campo**	a leenya də mayoo kangpoo
offside	**fora de jogo**	fora de zhawgoo
penalty area	**a grande área**	a grangdə ahreea
penalty kick	**o penalti**	oo penahltee
players	**os jogadores**	oosh zhoogadawrəsh
referee	**o árbitro**	oo ahrbeetroo
team	**a equipa**	a eekeepa
wing	**o flanco**	oo flangkoo

Race Meetings

I want a ticket for the paddock/for the grandstand, please.	**Queria um bilhete para o padoque/para a bancada, se fazia favor.**	kəreea oong beellyehtə para oo pahdokə/para a bangkahda sə fazeea favawr
Where can I place a bet?	**Aonde é que posso apostar?**	aawngde e kə posoo apooshtahr
What are the odds on number 5?	**Quais são as probabilidades do número cinco ganhar?**	kooysh sowng ash proobableedahdəsh doo noomaroo seengkoo ganyahr
I'd like to back it	**Queria apostar nele**	kəreea apooshtahr nehlə
to win.	**para ganhar**	para gahnyahr
each way.	**para primeiro, segundo e terceiro lugar.**	para preemayroo segoongdoo e tersayroo lugahr
for a place.	**para segundo ou terceiro.**	para segoongdoo aw tersayroo
Which is the favourite?	**Qual e o favorito?**	kooahl e oo favoreetoo
I will back the outsider.	**Vou apostar no desconhecido.**	vaw apooshtahr noo dəshkoonyəseedoo
Is the jockey well known?	**O jóquei é muito conhecido?**	oo zhokay e mooeengtoo koonyəseedoo?

Vocabulary

course	**a pista**	a peeshta
filly	**a poldra**	a pawldra
flat	**a reta**	a rreta
horse	**o cavalo**	oo kavahloo

hurdles	**os obstáculos**	oosh obshtahkooloosh
jockey	**o jóquei**	oo zhokay
owner	**o dono**	oo dawnoo
photo finish	**resultado comprovado por fotografia**	rrəzooltahdoo kawngproovahdoo poor footoografeea
rails	**o gradeamento**	oo gradeeamehngtoo
stable	**o estábulo**	oo əshtahbooloo
starting gate	**a partida**	a parteeda
tote	**o totalizador**	oo tootaleezadawr
trainer	**o treinador**	oo traynadawr

Tennis

Are there tennis courts near here?	**Há campos de ténis aqui perto?**	ah kangpoosh də tenees akee pertoo
Can I hire rackets?	**Posso alugar raquetas?**	posoo aloogahr rrahketash
Where is the championship being held?	**Aonde é que é o campeonato?**	aawngde e kə e oo kangpeeoonahtoo
How can I get some tickets?	**Como é que posso comprar bilhetes?**	kawmoo e kə posoo kawngprahr bəllyehtəsh
Should I arrive early?	**É preciso chegar cedo?**	e prəseezoo shəgahr sehdoo
Who is playing?	**Quem é que está a jogar?**	kayng e kə əshtah a zhoogahr
Is it on hard courts or grass?	**Os cortes são de terra batida ou de relva?**	oosh kortəsh sowng də terra bateeda aw də rrelva
I want to watch the men's singles/doubles/mixed doubles.	**Quero ver as partidas individuais de homens/os pares/os pares mistos.**	keroo vehr ash parteedash eengdəveedooysh də omehngsh/oosh pahrəsh/oosh pahrəsh meeshtoosh

How do you score in Portuguese?	**Como é que se diz os pontos em português?** kawmoo e kə sə deesh oosh **pawng**toosh ayng poortoogehsh
15, 30, 40, deuce, advantage in/out, game, set, match.	**Quinze, trinta, quarenta, igual, vantagem do serviço/da resposta, jogo, set, partida.** **keeng**zə, **treeng**ta, kooa**rehng**ta, eegooahl, vang**tah**zhayng doo sər**vee**soo/da rrəsh**posh**ta, **zhaw**goo, set, par**tee**da
Shall we toss for service?	**Vamos tirar à sorte para ver quem é que bola?** va**moosh** tee**rahr** ah **sort**ə para vehr kayng e ke **bola**
Let's adjust the net.	**Vamos ajustar a rede.** va**moosh** azhoosh**tahr** a **rehd**ə
It's too high/too low.	**Está alta demais/baixa demais.** əsh**tah** **ahl**ta də**mysh**/**bysh**a də**mysh**
That was out/in/on the line.	**Essa foi fora/dentro/bateu na linha.** **esa** foy **fora**/**dehng**troo/bate**hoo** na **leeny**a
Good shot.	**Boa bola.** **bawa** **bola**
Will you keep the score?	**Quer ser árbitro?** ker sehr **ahr**beetroo
Change ends.	**Mudem de campo.** **moo**dayng də **kang**poo

Vocabulary

backhand	**à direita**	a dee**rayta**
forehand	**à esquerda**	a əsh**kehr**da
racquet	**a raqueta**	a rrah**ket**a
rally	**o rally**	oo **rally**
smash	**puxar**	poo**shahr**
spin	**cortar**	koor**tahr**
tennis ball	**a bola de ténis**	a **bola** də **tenees**
umpire	**o árbitro**	oo **ahr**beetroo
volley	**o volley**	oo **volee**

Golf

Is there a golf course near by?	**Há um campo de golfe aqui perto?** ah oong kangpoo də golfə akee pertoo
Does one have to be a member?	**É preciso ser sócio?** e prəseezoo sehr soseeoo
Is there temporary membership?	**Aceitam sócios temporários?** asaytang soseeoosh tehngpoorahreeoosh
How much does it cost to 'play?	**Quanto é que custa jogar?** kooangtoo e kə kooshta zhoogahr?
I'd like a caddy.	**Queria um caddy.** kəreea oong kadee
Are there any trolleys for hire?	**Alugam carrinhos?** aloogang karreenyoosh
I'd like to speak to the professional.	**Queria falar com o instructor.** kəreea falahr kawng oo eengshtrootawr
Could you give me a lesson?	**Podia dar-me uma aula?** poodeea dahr-mə ooma owla
Will you play a round with me?	**Quer jogar comigo?** ker zhoogahr koomeegoo
My handicap is eighteen.	**O meu handicap é dezoito.** oo mehoo angdeekahp e dezoytoo
My drive is not long enough.	**Os meus drives não são suficientemente compridos.** oosh mehoosh drives nowng sowng soofəsee-ehngtəmehngtə kawngpreedoosh
My approach shots are weak.	**As minhas tacadas de approach são fracas.** ash meenyash takahdash də approach sowng frahkash
I'll do some putting while I wait for you.	**Vou practicar ·uns putts enquanto espero por si.** vaw prateekahr oongsh putts ehngkooangtoo əshperoo poor see

Can I hire some clubs?	**Posso alugar tacos?**	
	posoo aloogahr tahkoosh	
May I have a scorecard?	**Dá-me um cartão para marcar os pontos?**	
	dah-mə oong kartowng para markahr oosh pawngtoosh	

VOCABULARY

birdie	o birdie	oo birdie
bunker	a areia	a araya
club house	o clube	oo kloobə
eagle	o eagle	oo eagle
fairway	o relvado	oo rrelvahdoo
golf bag	o saco de golfe	oo sahkoo də golfə
green	o green	oo green
irons	os tacos	oosh tahkoosh
mashie	o mashie	oo mashie
niblick	o taco pequeno	oo tahkoo pəkehnoo
par	o par	oo pahr
rough	o terreno desigual	oo terrehnoo dəzeegooahl
tee	o montículo	oo mawngteekooloo

Water Skiing

I have never skiied before.	**Nunca fiz esqui.**	
	noongka feesh əskee	
I am not a good swimmer.	**Não sei nadar muito bem.**	
	nowng say nadahr mooeengtoo bayng	
Do I wear a life jacket?	**Visto um colete de salvação?**	
	veeshtoo oong koolehtə də sahlvasowng	
Will you please help me to put on the skis?	**Ajuda-me a pôr os esquis se faz favor?**	
	azhooda-mə a pawr oosh əskeesh sə fahsh favawr	
Please pass me the rope.	**Passa-me a corda se faz favor.**	
	pahsa-mə a korda sə fahsh favawr	

May I ride on the speed boat?	**Posso ir no barco?**	posoo eer noo bahrkoo
Can I borrow a wetsuit?	**Empresta-me um fato de borracha?**	eengpreshta-mə oong fahtoo də boorrahsha
I'm ready now.	**Já estou pronto(a).**	zha əshtaw prawngtoo(ta)
Just a moment.	**Um momento.**	oong momehngtoo

Vocabulary

aquaplane	**aquaplaning**	akooaplaneeng
bathing hat	**a touca de banho**	a tawka də banyoo
course	**a pista**	a peeshta
goggles	**os óculos de mergulho**	oosh okooloosh də mergoollyoo
jump	**o salto**	oo sahltoo
monoski	**mono**	mono
slalom	**slalom**	slaahləm

Riding

Is there a riding stable here?	**Há um centro hípico aqui?**	ah oong sehngtroo eepeekoo akee
Can I hire a horse for riding?	**Posso alugar um cavalo para montar?**	posoo aloogahr oong kavahloo para mawngtahr
Do you give lessons?	**Dão aulas?**	downg owlash
I'd like to go for a ride.	**Queria dar uma volta a cavalo.**	kəreea dahr ooma volta a kavahloo
I'd like a quiet horse.	**Queria um cavalo sossegado.**	kəreea oong kavahloo soosəgahdoo

Have you any ponies?	**Tem póneis?**	
	tehng ponaysh	
Will an instructor accompany the ride?	**O instructor vai-nos acompanhar?**	
	oo eengshtrootawr vy noosh akawngpanyahr	
I'd like to practise jumping.	**Queria practicar uns saltos.**	
	kəreea prateekahr oongsh sahltoosh	
I am an experienced rider.	**Tenho muita práctica de montar.**	
	tenyoo mooeengta prahteeka de mawngtahr	
I am a novice.	**Tenho pouca práctica de montar.**	
	tenyoo pawka prahteeka de mawngtahr	
Do you have English saddles?	**Tem selins inglêses?**	
	tehng səleengsh eenglehzəsh	
This horse has gone lame.	**Este cavalo está manco.**	
	ehshtə kavahloo əshtah mangkoo	
The girth is too loose.	**A cilha está larga demais.**	
	a seellya əshtah lahrga dəmysh	
Will you please adjust my stirrups?	**Pode-me ajustar os estribos por favor?**	
	podə-mə azhooshtahr oosh əshtreeboosh poor favawr	
Will you hold my horse while I get on?	**Pode segurar o cavalo enquanto eu monto?**	
	podə səgoorahr oo kavahloo ehngkooangtoo ehoo mawngtoo	
Will you give me a leg up?	**Ajuda-me a montar?**	
	azhooda-mə a mawngtahr	

VOCABULARY

bit	**o freio**	oo frayoo
blinkers	**os antolhos**	oosh angtawllyoosh
bridle	**a cabeçada**	a kabəsahda
gelding	**o cavalo castrado**	oo kavahloo kashtrahdoo
girth	**a cilha**	a seellya
harness	**o arreio**	oo arrayoo

hock	**o jarrete**	oo zharrehtə
hoof	**o casco**	oo kahshkoo
mare	**a égua**	a egooa
martingale	**a chibata**	a sheebahta
pony	**o pónei**	oo ponay
reins	**a rédea**	a rredeea
saddle	**o selim**	oo səling
stallion	**o garanhão**	oo garanyowng
withers	**as cernelhas**	ash sərnellyash

Fishing

Where can I get a permit to fish?
Aonde é que se arranja uma licença de pesca?
aawngde e kə sə arrangzha ooma leesehngsa də peshka

Are there places for fishing in this area?
Há sítios para pescar nesta área?
ah seeteeoosh para pəshkahr neshta ahreea

Are there any trout or salmon?
Há trutas ou salmão?
ah trootash aw sahlmowng

How much does a day's fishing cost?
Quanto é que custa pescar durante um dia?
kooangtoo e kə kooshta pəshkahr doorangtə oong deea

Is that per rod?
Esse é o preço por cabeça?
ehsə e oo prehsoo poor kabehsa

Where can I get some bait?
Aonde é que posso comprar isca?
aawngde e kə posoo kawngprahr eeshka

Is there a minimum size that I am allowed to keep?
Há alguma regra quanto ao tamanho mínimo de peixe que se pode pescar?
ah algooma rregra kooangtoo ow tamanyoo meeneemoo də payshə kə sə podə pəshkahr

What is the best time of day for fishing?
Qual é a melhor hora para pescar?
kooahl e a məllyor ora para pəshkahr

Are there any boats that will take me deep-sea fishing?
Há algum barco que me leve a fazar caça submarina?
ah algoong bahrkoo kə mə levə a fazehr kahsa soobmareena

Do they provide tackle?	**Eles fornecem o equipamento?**	ehləsh foornesayng oo eekeepamehngtoo

VOCABULARY

(to) cast	**lançar**	langsahr
dry/wet fly	**isca morta/viva**	eeshka morta/veeva
fishing season	**a época de pesca**	a epooka də peshka
flippers	**as barbatanas**	ash barbatanash
float	**o flutuador**	oo flootooadawr
gaff	**a gafa**	a gahfa
goggles	**os óculos de mergulho**	oosh okooloosh də mərgoollyoo
hook	**o anzol**	oo angzol
line	**a linha**	a leenya
lure	**a isca**	a eeshka
net	**a rede**	a rrehdə
oxygen cylinders	**as garrafas de oxigénio**	ash garrahfash də okseezheneeoo
reel	**o carrete**	oo karrehtə
snorkel	**o cano respirador**	oo kanoo rrəshpeeradawr
spinner	**o fiandeiro**	oo feeangdayroo
weights	**os pesos**	oosh pehzoosh
wetsuit	**o fato de borracha**	oo fahtoo də boorrahsha

Shooting

Where can I shoot?	**Aonde é que posso caçar?**	aawngde e kə posoo kasahr
Do I need a licence?	**Preciso de licença?**	prəseezoo də leesehngsa
I'd like to hire a 12-bore shotgun.	**Queria alugar uma espingarda calibre doze.**	kəreea aloogahr ooma əshpeenggahrda kaleebrə dawzə
I have my own rifle.	**Tenho a minha própria espingarda.**	tenyoo a meenya propreea əshpeenggahrda

Is there a shooting party I could join?	**Posso-me juntar a algum grupo de caçadores?** posoo-mə zhoongtahr a ahlgoong groopoo də kasadawrəsh
Is there a clay pigeon shoot?	**Fazem tiro aos pratos?** fazayng teeroo owsh prahtoosh
Is there a rifle range near?	**Há um campo de tiro aqui perto?** ah oong kangpoo də teeroo akee pertoo

Vocabulary

backsight	a alça	a ahlsa
barrel	o cano	oo kanoo
bullets	as balas	ash bahlash
butt	a coronha	a koorawnya
cartridges	os cartuchos	oosh kartooshoosh
ejector	o ejetor	oo eezhetawr
foresight	a mira	a meera
hammer	o cão	oo kowng
revolver	o revólver	oo rəvolvər
safety catch	a segurança	a səgoorangsa
telescopic sight	a mira telescópica	a meera tələshkopeeka
trigger	o gatilho	oo gateellyoo

Sailing and Boating

Is there a boat hire agent here?	**Há aqui uma agência de aluguer de barcos?** ah akee ooma azhehngseea də alooger də bahrkoosh
I'd like to hire a dinghy/a boat.	**Quero alugar um barco pequeno/um barco.** keroo aloogahr oong bahrkoo pəkehnoo/oong bahrkoo
Is an outboard motor extra?	**Um motor de fora de bordo custa extra?** oong mootawr də fora də bordo kooshta ayshtra
Does this have an auxiliary engine?	**Este barco tem motor auxiliar?** ehshtə bahrkoo tehng mootawr owseeleeahr

How many berths are there?	**Quantas camas tem?**	kooangtash kamash tehng
How much water does it draw?	**Quanta água é que mete?**	kooangta ahgooa e kə metə
Is there a stove/a sink/a chemical toilet?	**Há um fogão/um lava-louça/uma retrete química?**	ah oong foogowng/oong lahva lawsa/ooma rrətretə keemeeka
Are all cutlery, china and cooking utensils included?	**Inclui talheres, louça e utensilios para a cozinha?**	eengklooee tallyerəsh, lawsa ee ootehngseeleeoosh para a koozeenya
Are sheets and blankets provided?	**Fornecem lençóis e cobertores?**	foornesayng lehngsoysh ee koobərtawrəsh
Have you got a map of the river?	**Tem um mapa do rio?**	tehng oong mahpa doo rreeoo
How far is it to the next place where I can get fuel?	**Qual é a distância até ao próximo posto de gasolina?**	kooahl e a dəshtangseea ate ow proseemoo pawshtoo də gazooleena
Can I leave the boat here while we go to the shops?	**Posso deixar o barco aqui enquanto vamos as lojas?**	posoo dayshahr oo bahrkoo akee ehngkooangtoo vamoosh ahsh lozhash
Where is the next refuse dump?	**Aonde é a próxima lixeira?**	aawngde e a proseema leeshayra
I have run aground.	**Encalhei.**	ehngkallyay
Will you please give me a tow?	**Podia-me rebocar se faz favor?**	podeea-mə rəbookahr sə fahsh favawr

Vocabulary

anchor	**a âncora**	a angkoora
boat	**o barco**	oo bahrkoo

boathook	o croque	oo krokə
bow	a proa	a prawa
buoy	o bóia	a boeea
canoe	a canoa	a kanawa
chart	o roteiro	oo rrootayroo
coast	a costa	a koshta
current	a corrente	a koorrehngtə
deck	o deque	oo dekə
diesel engine	o motor diesel/gás óleo	oo mootawr deezəl/gash oleeoo
dinghy	o barco pequeno	oo bahrkoo pəkehnoo
fender	a defensa	a dəfehngsa
gale warning	o aviso de tempestade	oo aveezoo de tehngpəshtahdə
halyard	a adriça	a adreesa
hull	o casco	oo kahshkoo
jib	a vela da bujarrona	a vela da boozharrawna
keel	a quilha	a keellya
(to) leak	meter água	metehr ahgooa
lifebelt	o cinto de salvação	oo seengtoo də salvasowng
lifejacket	o colete de salvação	oo koolehtə də salvasowng
mainsail	a vela grande	a vela grangdə
mast	o mastro	oo mahshtroo
mooring	a amarra	a amahrra
motorboat	o gasolina	oo gazooleena
oar	o remo	oo rremoo
outboard motor	o motor de fora de bordo	oo motawr də fora də bordo
paddle	o remo	oo rremoo
pennant	o galhardete	oo gallyardehtə
port (left)	bombordo	bawngbordo
propeller	a hélice	a eleesə
rocks	as rochas	ash rroshash
rowing boat	o barco a remos	oo bahrkoo a rremoosh
sail	a vela	a vela
shallow	pouco profundo	pawkoo proofoongdoo

sheets	os lençóis	oosh lehngsoysh
starboard (right)	estibordo	əshteebordoo
(to) steer	navegar	navəgahr
stern	a popa	a pawpa
storm	a tempestade	a tehngpəshtahdə
tiller	a cana do leme	a kana doo lemə
wind	o vento	oo vehngtoo
yacht	o iate	oo eeahtə

General Services

If you are travelling independently or having a self-catering holiday at a villa or apartment, phrases for dealing with gas, electricity and plumbing problems will be indispensable. But even when that is taken care of by someone else, it is useful to be able to communicate with Post Office staff, telephone operators and other officials in their own language.

Post Office

Post offices in Portugal are called **correios** and their mail boxes are red. Stamps can also be bought at some stationers and newspaper shops.

Where is the nearest post office?	**Aonde é que é o correio mais próximo?** aawngde e kə e oo koorrayoo mysh proseemoo
What are the opening hours?	**A que horas abre?** a kə orash ahbrə
Can I cash an international money order here?	**Posso trocar um vale postal internacional aqui?** posoo trookahr oong vahlə pooshtahl eengtərnaseeonahl akee
I want some stamps for a letter to Britain.	**Quero sêlos para uma carta para a Grã-Bretanha.** keroo sehloosh para ooma kahrta para a grang-bretanya
What is the postcard postage rate for the USA?	**Quanto é que custa um sêlo de postal para os Estados Unidos?** kooangtoo e kə kooshta oong sehloo də pooshtahl para oosh əshtahdoosh ooneedoosh
I'd like to register this letter.	**Queria registar esta carta.** kəreea rrəzheeshtahr eshta kahrta
I want to send it by air-mail/express/surface/printed matter rate.	**Quero mandá-la por via aérea/expresso/pelo correio normal/como impresso.** keroo mangdah-la poor veea aereea/əshpresoo/pehloo koorrayoo normal/kawmoo eengpresoo

| Where do I post parcels? | **Aonde é que se despacham encomendas?** |
| | aawngde e kə sə dəshpahshang ehngkoomehngdash |

| Do I need a customs form? | **Preciso de um formulário de alfândega?** |
| | prəseezoo də oong foormoolahreeoo də ahlfangdəga |

| Is there a poste restante here? | **Há aqui posta restante?** |
| | ah akee poshta rrəshtangtə |

| Have you a letter for me? | **Tem uma carta para mim?** |
| | tehng ooma kahrta para meeng |

| May I have a telegram form? | **Dá-me um impresso de telegrama?** |
| | dah-mə oong eengpresoo də tələgrama |

| I'll send it by the cheap rate/ at the normal rate. | **Vou mandar pela tarifa mais barata/ pela tarifa normal.** |
| | vaw mangdahr pehla tareefa mysh barahta/pehla tareefa normahl |

| When will it arrive? | **Quando é que chega?** |
| | kooangdoo e kə shehga |

I want to make	**Quero fazer**
	keroo fazehr
a local call.	**uma chamada local.**
	ooma shamahda lookahl
an international call.	**uma chamada internacional.**
	ooma shamahda eengtərnaseeoonahl
a person-to-person call.	**uma chamada pessoal.**
	ooma shamahda pesooahl

| Can I make a reverse-charge call? | **Posso telefonar e mandar pagar no destino?** |
| | posoo tələfoonahr ee mangdahr pagahr noo dəshteenoo |

| Switchboard, the line is engaged. Please try again later. | **Minha senhora, o número está impedido. Pode voltar a ligar mais tarde, por favor.** |
| | meenya sənyawra, oo noomeroo əshtah eengpədeedoo. podə voltahr a leegahr mysh tahrdə poor favawr |

The Police Station

I am a visitor to your country.	**Estou de visita ao seu país.** əshtaw də vəzeeta ow sehoo paeesh
I want to report	**Quero comunicar** keroo koomooneekahr
a theft.	**um roubo.** oong rrawboo
a loss.	**uma perca.** ooma perka
an accident.	**um acidente.** oong aseedehngtə
Someone stole my wallet.	**Alguem roubou a minha carteira.** ahlgayng rrawbaw a meenya kartayra
Something was stolen from my car/my hotel room.	**Roubaram uma coisa do carro/do meu quarto de hotel.** rawbahrang ooma koyza doo kahrroo/ doo mehoo kooahrtoo də otel
The theft occurred in Rua Castilho at about 4 o'clock.	**O roubo deu-se na Rua Castilho por volta das quatro horas.** oo rrawboo dehoo-sə na rrooa kashteellyoo poor volta dash kooahtroo orash
I have lost my watch on the beach.	**Perdi o meu relógio na praia.** pərdee oo mehoo rrəlozheeoo na prya
It is valuable.	**É valioso.** e valeeawzoo
It has sentimental value.	**Tem valor sentimental.** tehng valawr sehngteemehngtahl
I will offer a reward.	**Vou oferecer uma recompensa.** vaw ofrəsehr ooma rrəkawngpehngsa
Someone has been knocked down.	**Alguem foi atropelado.** ahlgayng foy atroopəlahdoo

A lady has broken her leg.	**Uma senhora partiu a perna.**
	ooma senyawra parteeoo a perna

I have been swindled.	**Fui aldrabado(a).**
	fooee ahldrabahdoo(a)

Can a police officer come with me?	**Um agente da polícia pode acompanhar-me?**
	oong azhehngtə da pooleeseea podə akawngpanyahr-mə

I will be a witness.	**Eu sirvo de testemunha.**
	ehoo seervoo də təshtəmoonya

I cannot be a witness. I did not see what was happening.	**Não posso ser testemunha. Não vi o que se passou.**
	nowng posoo sehr təshtəmoonya. nowng vee oo kə sə pasaw

Is there anyone who speaks English?	**Há aqui alguém que fale inglês?**
	ah akee ahlgayng kə fahlə eengglehsh

Electricity

The lights have gone out.	**As luzes apagaram-se.**
	ash loozəsh apagahrang-sə

The power plug is not working.	**A tomada não funciona.**
	a toomahda nowng foongseeawna

The fuse has gone.	**Rebentou-se o fusível.**
	rrəbehngtaw-sə oo foozeevel

I think it's the switch.	**Acho que é o interruptor.**
	ashoo kə e oo eengtərrooptawr

There is a smell of burning.	**Cheira a queimado.**
	shayra a kaymahdoo

The stove won't light.	**O fogão não acende.**
	oo foogowng nowng asehngdə

The heating isn't working.	**O aquecimento não funciona.**
	oo akeseemehngtoo nowng foongseeawna

Can you mend it straight away?	**Pode arranjá-lo já?** podə arrangzhah-loo zhah
Where is the fuse box?	**Aonde é o quadro dos fusíveis?** aawngde e oo kooahdroo doosh foozeevaysh
Where is the main switch?	**Aonde é o interruptor principal?** aawngde e oo eengtərrooptawr preengseepahl

VOCABULARY

adaptor	**o transformador**	oo trangshfoormadawr
bulb	**a lâmpada**	a langpada
electric cooker	**o fogão eléctrico**	oo foogowng eeletreekoo
electric fire	**o aquecedor eléctrico**	oo akesədawr eeletreekoo
extension lead	**a extensão**	a əshtehngsowng
fuse wire	**o fio do fusível**	oo feeoo doo foozeevel
hair dryer	**o secador**	oo səkadawr
immersion heater	**o esquentador**	oo əshkehngtadawr
insulating tape	**a fita isoladora**	a feeta eezooladawra
iron	**o ferro**	oo ferroo
oven	**o forno**	oo fawrnoo
plug	**a tomada**	a tomahda
radio	**o rádio**	oo rrahdeeoo
razor point	**a ficha para a máquina**	a feesha para a mahkeena
refrigerator	**o frigorífico**	oo freegooreefeekoo
spotlight	**o holofote**	oo olofotə
television	**a televisão**	a tələveezowng
torch	**a lanterna**	a langterna

Gas

| There is a smell of gas. | **Cheira a gás.** shayra a gahsh |
| It must be a gas leak. | **Deve ser uma fuga de gás.** devə sehr ooma fooga de gahsh |

This is the gas meter. **Este é o contador do gás.**
ehshtə e oo kawngtadawr doo gahsh

The gas jet won't light. **O piloto não acende.**
oo peelawtoo nowng asehngdə

The pilot light won't stay on. **O piloto apaga-se.**
oo peelawtoo apahga-sə

Is there any danger of an explosion? **Há perigo de explosão?**
ah pəreegoo də əshploozowng

I think the ventilator is blocked. **Acho que o ventilador está entupido.**
ahshoo kə oo vehngteeladawr əshtah ehngtoopeedoo

We can't get any hot water. **Não temos água quente.**
nowng tehmoosh ahgooa kehngtə

VOCABULARY

chimney	a chaminé	a shameene
gas fire	o fogão a gás	oo foogowng a gahsh
gas light	o piloto do gás	oo peelawtoo doo gahsh
gas pipe	o cano do gás	oo kanoo doo gahsh
gas tap	a torneira do gás	a toornayra doo gahsh
geyser	o esquentador	oo əshkehngtadawr
hammer	o martelo	oo marteloo
key	a chave	a shahvə
lagging	o material isolador	oo matəreeahl eezooladawr
monkey wrench	a chave inglesa	a shahvə eengglehza
spanner	a chave de porcas	a shahvə də porkash

Plumbing

Are you the plumber? **O senhor é o canalizador?**
oo senyawr e oo kanaleezadawr

The sink is stopped up. **O lava-louça está entupido.**
oo lahva lawsa əshtah ehngtoopeedoo

| There is a blockage in the pipe. | **O cano está entupido.** |
| | oo kanoo əshtah ehngtoopeedoo |

| The tap is dripping. | **A torneira está a pingar.** |
| | a toornayra əshtah a peengahr |

| The tap needs a new washer. | **A torneira precisa de uma anilha nova.** |
| | a toornayra prəseeza dooma aneellya nova |

| This water pipe is leaking. | **Este cano de água está a pingar.** |
| | ehshtə kanoo də ahgooa əshtah a peenggahr |

| The lavatory cistern won't fill. | **O autoclismo da retrete não enche.** |
| | oo owtookleesmoo da rrətretə nowng ehngshə |

| The valve is stuck. | **A válvula está encravada.** |
| | a vahlvoola əshtah ehngkravahda |

| The float is punctured. | **O flutoador está furado.** |
| | oo flootooadawr əshtah foorahdoo |

| The tank is overflowing. | **O tanque está a deitar por fora.** |
| | oo tangkə əshtah a daytahr poor fora |

| The water tank has run dry. | **O tanque está seco.** |
| | oo tangkə əshtah sehkoo |

VOCABULARY

basin	**o lavatório**	oo lavatoreeoo
bath	**a banheira**	a banyayra
cesspool	**a fossa**	a fosa
drain	**o esgoto**	oo əshgawtoo
immersion heater	**o esquentador**	oo əshkehngtadawr
main drainage	**o esgoto principal**	oo əshgawtoo preengseepahl
mains water	**a água canalizada**	a ahgooa kanaleezahda
overflow pipe	**o cano de escoamento**	oo kanoo de əshkooamehngtoo
plug	**a tampa**	a tangpa
stopcock	**a chave de fonte**	a shahvə də fawngtə

Personal Services

This section suggests useful phrases for such occasions as a visit to a doctor, dentist, hairdresser or beautician.

At the Doctor's

Can you recommend a doctor?	**Pode-me recomendar um médico?** podə-mə rrəkoomehngdahr oong medeekoo
Is there an English-speaking doctor in the resort?	**Há um médico que fala inglês aqui?** ah oong medeekoo kə fahla eengglehsh akee
Where is the surgery?	**Aonde é o consultório?** aawngde e oo kawngsooltoreeoo
I have an appointment.	**Tenho consulta marcada.** tenyoo kawngsoolta markahda
My name is...	**O meu nome e...** oo mehoo nawmə e...
Can the doctor come to the hotel/house?	**O médico pode vir ao hotel/a casa?** oo medeekoo podə veer ow otel/a kahza
I'm not feeling well.	**Não me sinto bem.** nowng me seengtoo bayng
I feel	**Estou** əshtaw
sick.	**enjoado(a).** ehngzhooahdoo(a)
dizzy.	**tonto(a).** tawngtoo(a)
faint.	**a desmaiar.** a dəshmyahr
shivery.	**com calafrios.** kawng kalafreeoosh

I have	**Tenho**
	tenyoo
a temperature.	**febre.**
	febrə
a headache.	**dores de cabeça.**
	dawrəsh de kabehsa
back ache.	**dores de costas.**
	dawrəsh də koshtash
a sore throat.	**dores de garganta.**
	dawrəsh də gargangta
sunburn.	**queimaduras do sol.**
	kaymadoorash doo sol
diarrhoea.	**diarreia.**
	deearraya

I am constipated.	**Tenho prisão de ventre.**
	tehnyoo preezowng də vehngtrə
The pain is here.	**A dor é aqui.**
	a dawr e akee
I have been vomiting.	**Tenho vomitado.**
	tenyoo voomeetahdoo
I have hurt my...	**Magoei o meu (a minha)...**
	magooay oo mehoo (a meenya)
I have been like this since yesterday.	**Estou assim desde ontem.**
	əshtaw aseeng dehshdə awngtayng
Do you want me to take my clothes off?	**Quer que me dispa?**
	ker kə mə deeshpa
Is it serious?	**É grave?**
	e grahvə
Should I stay in bed?	**Devo ficar na cama?**
	dehvoo feekahr na kama
Should I arrange to go home?	**Devo voltar ao meu país?**
	dehvoo voltar ow mehoo paeesh

I am allergic to...	**Sou alérgico(a) a...**	
	saw alerzheekoo(a) a...	
I have a heart condition.	**Sofro do coração.**	
	sawfroo doo koorasowng	
I am asthmatic/ diabetic.	**Sou asmático(a)/diabético(a).**	
	saw ashmahteekoo(a)/deeabeteekoo(a)	
I am pregnant.	**Estou grávida.**	
	əshtaw grahveeda	
Do I have to pay for hospitalization and medicines?	**Tenho que pagar o hospital e os remédios?**	
	tehnyoo kə pagahr oo oshpeetahl ee oosh rrəmedeeoosh	

VOCABULARY

PARTS OF THE BODY

ankle	**o tornozelo**	oo toornoozehloo
appendix	**o apêndice**	oo apehngdeesə
arm	**o braço**	oo brahsoo
artery	**a artéria**	a artereea
back	**as costas**	ash koshtash
bladder	**a bexiga**	a bəsheega
blood	**o sangue**	oo sangguə
bone	**o osso**	oo awsoo
bowels	**os intestinos**	oosh eengtəshteenoosh
breast	**o peito**	oo paytoo
cheek	**a bochecha**	a booshaysha
chest	**o peito**	oo paytoo
chin	**o queixo**	oo kayshoo
collar bone	**a clavícula**	a klaveekoola
ear	**a orelha**	a orellya
elbow	**o cotovelo**	oo kootoovehloo
eye	**o olho**	oo awllyoo
face	**a cara**	a kahra
finger	**o dedo**	oo dehdoo

foot	o pé	oo pe
forehead	a testa	a teshta
gland	a glândula	a glangdoola
hand	a mão	a mowng
head	a cabeça	a kabehsa
heart	o coração	oo koorasowng
heel	o calcanhar	oo kahlkanyahr
hip	a anca	a angka
intestine	o intestino	oo eengtəshteenoo
jaw	o maxilar	oo mahkseelahr
joint	a articulação	a arteekoolasowng
kidney	o rim	oo reeng
knee	o joelho	oo zhooellyoo
leg	a perna	a perna
lip	o lábio	oo lahbeeoo
liver	o fígado	oo feegadoo
lung	o pulmão	oo poolmowng
mouth	a boca	a bawka
muscle	o músculo	oo mooshkooloo
neck	o pescoço	oo pəshkawsoo
nerve	o nervo	oo nehrvoo
nose	o nariz	oo nareesh
penis	o pénis	oo peneesh
rib	a costela	a kooshtela
shoulder	o ombro	oo awngbroo
skin	a pele	a pelə
spine	a coluna	a kooloona
stomach	o estômago	oo əshtawmagoo
tendon	o tendão	oo tehngdowng
testicles	os testículos	oosh təshteekooloosh
thigh	a coxa	a kawsha
throat	a garganta	a gargangta
thumb	o polegar	oo poolgahr
toe	o dedo do pé	oo dehdoo doo pe
tongue	a lingua	a leenggooa
tonsils	as amígdalas	ash ameegdalash
urine	a urina	a ooreena
vagina	a vagina	a vazheena

vein	a veia	a vaya
womb	o útero	oo ootəroo
wrist	o pulso	oo poolsoo

INDISPOSITIONS

abscess	o abcesso	oo absesoo
appendicitis	a apendecite	a apehngdəseetə
arthritis	a artrite	a artreetə
asthma	a asma	a ahzhma
blisters	as bolhas	ash bawllyash
boil	o furúnculo	oo fooroongkooloo
bruise	a nódoa negra	a nodooa nehgra
	[a mancha roxa]	[a mangsha rrawsha]
chill	a constipação	a kawngshteepasowng
cold	a constipação	a kawngshteepasowng
	[o resfriado]	[oo rrəshfreeahdoo]
convulsions	as convulsões	ash kawngvoolsoyngsh
cramp	a cãibra	a kayngbra
cut	o corte	oo kortə
cyst	o quisto	oo keeshtoo
diabetes	os diabetes	oosh deeabetəsh
diarrhoea	a diarreia	a deearraya
dizziness	as tonturas	ash tawngtoorash
haemorrhoids	as hemorróidas	ash eemoorroeedash
hay fever	a febre de feno	a febrə də fehnoo
high/low blood pressure	tensão alta/baixa	tehngsowng ahlta/bysha
indigestion	a indigestão	a eengdəzhəshtowng
infection	a infecção	a eengfesowng
inflammation	a inflamação	a eengflamasowng
influenza	a gripe	a greepə
irritation	a inflamação	a eengflamasowng
nausea	o enjôo	oo ehngzhawoo
pneumonia	a pneumonia	a pnehoomooneea
rheumatism	o reumático	oo rrehoomahteekoo
scald	a queimadura	a kaymadoora

shivers	os calafrios	oosh kalafreeoosh
slipped disc	a hernia discal	a erneea deeshkahl
stiff neck	o torcicól	oo toorseekol
sting	a picada	a peekahda
sunstroke	a insolação	a eengsoolasowng
swelling	o inchaço	oo eengshahsoo
temperature	a febre	a febrə
tonsilitis	as anginas	ash angzheenash
ulcer	a úlcera	a oolsəra
whooping cough	a tosse convulsa	a tosə kawngvoolsa
wound	a ferida	a fəreeda

At the Dentist's

Can you recommend a dentist?	**Pode-me recomendar um dentista?**
	podə-mə rrəkoomehngdahr oong dehngteeshta
I need treatment as soon as possible.	**Preciso de ser tratado com urgência.**
	prəseezoo de sehr tratahdoo kawng oorzhehngseea
I have a toothache/ an abscess.	**Tenho dores de dentes/um abcesso.**
	tehnyoo dawrəsh də dehngtəsh/oong absesoo
I've lost a filling.	**Perdi um chumbo.**
	perdee oong shoongboo
My gums are bleeding/ my gums are sore.	**Estou a sangrar das gengivas/doiem-me as gengivas.**
	əshtaw a sanggrahr dash zhehngzheevash/doyayng-mə ash zhehngzheevash
I have broken my dentures.	**Parti a dentadura.**
	partee a dehngtadoora
Can you suggest a painkiller in the meantime?	**Pode-me recomendar um analgésico até lá?**
	podə-mə rrəkoomehngdahr oong anahlzhezeekoo ate lah

The bad tooth is	**O dente que me dói é**
	oo dehngtə kə mə doee e
at the front/back/ side.	**à frente/atrás/de lado.**
	ah frehngtə/atrahsh/də lahdoo
Can you extract it?	**Podo tirá-lo?**
	podə teerah-loo
Does it need filling?	**Precisa de um chumbo?**
	prəseeza də oong shoongboo
Can you put a temporary filling in?	**Pode pôr massa?**
	podə pawr mahsa
Can I bite normally?	**Posso trincar normalmente?**
	posoo treengkahr normahlmehngtə
I'd prefer gas to an injection.	**Prefiro gás a uma injecção.**
	prəfeeroo gahsh a ooma eenzhesowng
What is your fee?	**Quanto é que leva por consulta?**
	kooangtoo e kə leva poor kawngsoolta

At the Optician's

Can you recommend an optician?	**Pode-me recomendar um oculista?**
	podə-mə rrəkoomehngdahr oong okooleeshta
I have broken my glasses.	**Parti os óculos.**
	partee oosh okooloosh
Can you repair them temporarily?	**Pode fazer um arranjo temporário?**
	podə fazehr oong arrangzhoo tehngpoorahreeoo
The lens is broken. Can you get a new one quickly?	**A lente está partida. Pode arranjar-me uma nova rapidamente?**
	a lehngtə əshtah parteeda. podeea arrangzhahr-mə ooma nova rahpeedamehngtə
Have you got contact lenses?	**Tem lentes de contacto?**
	tehng lehngtəsh də kawngtahktoo

I'd like a pair of tinted spectacles.	**Queria uns óculos com lentes fumadas.** kəreea oongsh okooloosh kawng lehngtəsh foomahdash
Do you sell binoculars/ sunglasses?	**Tem binóculos/óculos escuros?** tehng beenokooloosh/okooloosh əshkooroosh
I had better have an eye test.	**É melhor fazer um teste à vista.** e məllyor fazehr oong teshtə ah veeshta
I am shortsighted/ long sighted.	**Sou miope/só vejo ao longe.** saw meeoopə/so vehzhoo ow lawngzhə
How long will it take to make me some new glasses?	**Quanto tempo demora a fazer-me uns óculos novos?** kooangtoo tehngpoo dəmora a fazehr-mə oongsh okooloosh novoosh
How much will they cost?	**Quanto é que vão custar?** kooangtoo e kə vowng kooshtahr

At the Chiropodist's

Can you recommend a chiropodist?	**Pode-me recomendar um calista?** podə-mə rrəkoomehngdahr oong kaleeshta
I have a painful corn.	**Tenho um calo doloroso.** tehnyoo oong kahloo doolooorawzoo
Can you remove it?	**Pode cortá-lo?** podə kortah-loo
My bunion is rubbing against my shoe.	**O calo no joanete roça contra o sapato.** oo kahloo noo zhooanehtə rrosa kawngtra oo sapahtoo
I have a hard spot on the ball of my foot.	**Tenho um ponto duro na sola do pé.** tehnyoo oong pawngtoo dooroo na sola doo pe
My nails need attention. One of them is ingrowing.	**Preciso que me trate das unhas. Uma delas está encravada.** prəseezoo kə mə trahtə dash oonyash. ooma delash əshtah ehngkravahda

Have you anything to soften them?

Tem algum produto para as amolecer?

tehng ahlgoong proodootoo para ash amoolƏsehr

The soles of my feet are very sore.

Estou com muitas dores nas solas dos pés.

Əshtaw kawng mooeengtash dawrƏsh nash solash doosh pesh

At the Hairdresser's

Where is the nearest hairdresser?

Onde é o cabeleireiro mais próximo?

awngde e oo kabƏlayrayroo mysh proseemoo

I'd like to make an appointment.

Queria fazer uma marcação.

kƏreea fazehr ooma markasowng

I'd like a shampoo and set, please.

Quero lavar a cabeça e pôr rolos.

keroo lavahr a kabehsa ee pawr rrawloosh

I want it cut, please.

Quero que o corte, se faz favor.

keroo kƏ oo kortƏ se fahsh favawr

I wear it brushed forward with a fringe.

Quero-o penteado para a frente com franja.

keroo-oo pehngteeahdoo para a frengtƏ kawng frangzha

I like it brushed back.

Gosto dele penteado para trás.

goshtoo dehlƏ pehngteeahdoo para trahsh

Can you put in some waves/some curls?

Pode fazer ondas/caracóis?

podƏ fazehr awngdash/karakoeesh

Brush it back into a bun, please.

Pode penteá-lo para trás e fazer um chignon por favor.

podƏ pehngteeah-loo para trahsh ee fazehr oong sheenawng poor favawr

I would like a colour rinse.

Queria pôr reflexos.

kƏreea pawr refleksoosh

I think I will have it dyed.

Acho que quero pintá-lo.

ahshoo kƏ keroo peengtah-loo

Have you a colour chart?

Tem uma amostra das cores?

tehng ooma amoshtra dash kawrƏsh

No hairspray, thank you.	**Não quero laca, obrigada.** nowng keroo lahka obreegahda	
I'd like a manicure.	**Queria arranjar as unhas.** kəreea arrangzhahr ash oonyash	
What is the name of this varnish?	**Como é que se chama este verniz?** kawmoo e kə sə shama ehshtə vərneesh	

Vocabulary

auburn	**castanho arruivado**	kashtanyoo arrooeevahdoo
blonde	**loiro**	loyroo
brunette	**moreno**	moorehnoo
brush	**a escova**	a əshkawva
comb	**o pente**	oo pehngtə
hairdryer	**o secador de cabelo**	oo səkadawr də kabehloo
hairnet	**a rede**	a rrehdə
hair piece	**o postiço**	oo pooshteesoo
hairpin	**o gancho**	oo gangshoo
razor	**a navalha**	a navahllya
rollers	**os rolos**	oosh rrawloosh
scissors	**a tesoura**	a təzawra
shampoo	**o champô**	oo shangpaw
(to) style	**dar forma/pentear**	dahr forma/pehngteahr
wig	**a perruca**	a pərrooka

At the Beauty Salon

I'd like	**Queria** kəreea	
a complete beauty treatment.	**um tratamento de beleza completo.** oong tratamehngtoo də bəlehza kawngpletoo	
just a facial.	**só na cara.** so na kahra	

I'd like to change my makeup.	**Queria mudar a minha maquiage.** kəreea moodahr a meenya mahkeellyahzhə
I'd like	**Queria** kəreea
something more suitable for the seaside.	**alguma coisa mais própria para a praia.** ahlgooma koyza mysh propreea para a prya
something lighter in tone.	**um tom mais claro.** oong tawng mysh klahroo
a more open-air look.	**uma maquiage mais natural.** ooma mahkeellyahzhə mysh natoorahl
something for the evening.	**maquiage para a noite.** mahkeellyahzhə para a noytə
I have a delicate skin.	**Tenho uma pele delicada.** tenyoo ooma pelə dəleekahda
Can you please suggest a new eye make-up?	**Pode-me sugerir uma maquiage nova para os olhos?** podə-mə soozhəreer ooma mahkeellyahzhə nova para oosh ollyoosh
I think that is too heavy.	**Acho que fica muito pesado.** ahshoo kə feeka mooeengtoo pəzahdoo
Have you any false eye-lashes?	**Tem pestanas postiças?** tehng pəshtanash pooshteesash
Perhaps my eyebrows need plucking.	**Talvez precise de arranjar as sobrancelhas.** tahlvehsh'prəseezə də arrangzhahr ash soobrangsellyash
I'd like to see some new lipstick colours.	**Queria vêr côres novas de batom.** kəreea vehr kawrəsh novash də batawng

At the Laundry/Cleaner's

I'd like them washed and pressed, please.	**Queria que os lavasse e engomasse, por favor.** kəreea kə oosh lavahsə ee eenggoomahsə poor favawr

Will you iron the shirts?	**Podia engomar estas camisas?**
	poodeea ehnggoomahr eshtash kameezash
I will collect them tomorrow.	**Venho buscá-los amanhã.**
	venyoo booshkah-loosh amanyang
Do you deliver?	**Fazem entregas?**
	fahzayng ehngtregash
Do you do mending?	**Fazem arranjos?**
	fahzayng arrangzhoosh
This tear needs patching.	**Este rasgão precisa de ser remendado.**
	ehshtə rrashgowng prəseeza də sehr rremehngdahdoo
Can you sew this button on?	**Podia-me pregar este botão?**
	poodeea-mə prəgahr ehshtə bootowng
Can you remove this stain? It is coffee/blood/grease/biro.	**Pode tirar esta nódoa? É de café/de sangue/de gordura/de esferográfica.**
	podə teerahr eshta nodooa? e də kafe/də sanggə/də goordoora/də əshferograhfeeka
Can you mend this invisibly?	**Pode serzir isto?**
	podə sərzeer eeshtoo
This blouse is not mine.	**Esta blusa não é minha.**
	eshta blooza nowng e meenya
This coat/this dress is not mine.	**Este casaco/este vestido não e meu.**
	ehshtə kazahkoo/ehshtə veshteedoo nowng e mehoo
My trousers are missing.	**Faltam as minhas calças.**
	fahltang ash meenyash kahlsash
This was not torn when I brought it to you.	**Isto não estava rasgado quando o entreguei.**
	eeshtoo nowng əshtahva rrashgahdoo koangdoo oo ehngtrəgay
How long does the launderette stay open?	**Até quando é que fica aberta a lavandaria?**
	ate kooangdoo e kə feeka aberta a lavangdareea

VOCABULARY

bleach	**a lixívia**	a ləsheeveea
(to) clean	**limpar**	leengpahr
cleaning fluid	**o tira nódoas**	oo teera nodooash
clothes hanger	**o cabide**	oo kabeedə
cold/ hot/ warm water	**água fria/ quente/ morna**	ahgooa freea/ kehngtə/ morna
dryer	**a máquina de secar**	a mahkeena də səkahr
launderette	**a lavandaria**	a lavangdareea
rinse	**passar por água**	pasahr poor ahgooa
soap powder	**o detergente**	oo dətərzhehngtə
(to) spin	**espremer**	əshprəmehr
(to) tumble dry	**secar na máquina**	sekahr na mahkeena
(the) washing	**a roupa**	a rrawpa
washing machine	**a máquina de lavar**	a mahkeena də lavahr

At the Men's Hairdresser

I want a haircut, please.	**Quero cortar o cabelo, se faz favor.** keroo koortahr oo kabehloo se fahsh favawr
Just a trim. I haven't much time.	**É só para aparar. Tenho pouco tempo.** e so para aparahr. tenyoo pawkoo tehngpoo
Please give me a shampoo.	**Lava-me a cabeça, se faz favor?** lahva-mə a kabehsa sə fahsh favawr
I would like it cut shorter.	**Queria mais curto.** kəreea mysh koortoo
Leave it long, please.	**Deixe-o comprido, por favor.** dayshə-oo kawngpreedoo poor favawr
You are taking too much off.	**Está a cortar demais.** əshtah a koortahr dəmysh

Please take a little more	**Por favor, podia cortar mais** poor favawr, poodeea koortahr'mysh
off the back.	**atrás.** atrahsh
off the sides.	**dos lados.** doosh lahdoosh
off the top.	**em cima.** ayng seema
I part my hair	**Faço risca** fahsoo rreeshka
on the left/on the right.	**do lado esquerdo/do lado direito.** doo lahdoo əshkehrdoo/doo lahdoo deeraytoo
I'd like an alcohol rub.	**Queria uma fricção de álcool.** kəreea ooma freeksowng də ahlkol
A singe, please.	**Queima-me as pontas, por favor.** kaymə-mə ash pawngtash poor favawr
Please give me a shave.	**Faz-me a barba, por favor.** fahsh-mə a bahrba poor favawr
Please trim my beard/moustache/sideboards.	**Pode-me aparar a barba/o bigode/as patilhas.** podə-mə aparahr a bahrba/oo beegodə/ash pateellyash
No thank you, I do not want a facial massage.	**Não obrigado, não quero uma massagem na cara.** nowng obreegahdoo, nowng keroo ooma masahzhayng na kahra
I will have a manicure.	**Quero arranjar as unhas.** keroo arrangzhahr ash oonyash
May I have a hand towel?	**Dáva-me uma toalha para as mãos?** dahva-mə ooma tooahllya para ash mowngsh
Put some eau de cologne on but no cream.	**Ponha água de colónia mas não ponha creme.** pawnya ahgooa də kooloneea mash nowng pawnya kremə

Can you please move
the mirror a bit more
to the right/to the left.

**Por favor, pode chegar o espelho um bocado à
direita/à esquerda.**
poor favawr, podə shəgahr oo eshpellyoo oong
bookahdoo ah deerayta/ah əshkehrda

Yes, that's fine.

Sim, assim está bem.
seeng, aseeng əshtah bayng

Making Friends

Good morning/good afternoon/good evening.	**Bom dia/boa tarde/boa tarde (boa noite.)** bawng deea/bawa tahrdə/bawa tahrdə/bawa noytə
May I introduce myself?	**Posso-me apresentar?** posoo-mə aprəzehngtahr
May I introduce my friend John?	**Posso apresentar o meu amigo John.** posoo aprəzehngtahr oo mehoo ameegoo John
May I introduce my wife?	**Posso apresentar a minha mulher?** posoo aprəzehngtahr a meenya moollyer
My name is...	**Chamo-me...** shamoo-mə
How do you do?	**Como está?** kawmoo əshtah
Are you staying at this hotel/at this resort?	**Está aqui neste hotel/nesta estância de férias?** əshtah akee nehshtə otel/nehshta əshtangseea də fereeash
Are you enjoying your holiday?	**Está a gostar das suas férias?** əshtah a gooshtahr dash sooash fereeash
How long have you been on holiday?	**Hà quanto tempo está de férias?** ah kooangtoo tehngpoo əshtah də fereeash
Do you always come here?	**Vem sempre para aqui?** vayng sehngprə para akee
I'd like you to meet my friend...	**Queria apresentá-lo ao meu amigo...** kəreea aprəzehngtah-loo ow mehoo ameegoo
Would you care to have a drink with me/us?	**Quer tomar uma bebida comigo/connosco?** ker toomahr ooma bəbeeda koomeegoo/kawngnawshkoo
What would you like?	**O que é que toma?** oo kə e kə toma

Please. I insist that you let me pay.	**Por favor. Insisto que me deixe pagar.**
	poor favawr. eengseeshtoo kə mə dayshə pagahr
I'm afraid that I don't speak Portuguese very well.	**Infelizmente não falo muito bem português.**
	eengfəleezhmehngte nowng fahloo mooeengtoo bayng poortoogehsh
It is very nice to talk to a Portuguese person.	**É muito agradável falar com uma pessoa portuguêsa.**
	e mooeengtoo agradahvel falahr kawng ooma pəsawa poortoogehsa
Which part of Portugal do you come from?	**É de que zona de Portugal?**
	e də kə zawna də poortoogahl
I am here with my	**Estou aqui com**
	əshtaw akee kawng
wife/husband/ family/friends.	**a minha mulher/o meu marido/a minha família/ os meus amigos.**
	a meenya moollyer/oo mehoo mareedoo/a meenya fameelea/oosh mehoosh ameegoosh
Are you alone?	**Está sòzinho(a)?**
	əshtah sozeenyoo(a)
We come from Ireland/England.	**Somos da Irlanda/de Inglaterra.**
	sawmoosh da eerlangda/də eengglaterra
Have you been to England?	**Já esteve em Inglaterra?**
	zhah əshtehvə ayng eengglaterra
If you come, please let me know.	**Se vier, avise-me.**
	sə vee-er aveezə-mə
This is my address.	**Esta é a minha morada**
	eshta e a meenya moorahda
I hope to see you again soon.	**Espero voltar a vê-lo em breve.**
	eshperoo voltahr a veh-loo ayng brevə
Perhaps you would like to meet for a drink after dinner?	**Talvez nos pudéssemos encontrar para tomar uma bebida depois do jantar?**
	tahlvehsh noosh poodesəmoosh ehngkawngtrahr para toomahr ooma bəbeeda dəpoysh doo zhangtahr

I would be delighted to join you.	**Com todo o prazer.** kawng tawdoo oo prazehr
When should we meet?	**A que horas é que nos encontramos?** a kə orash e kə noosh ehngkawngtramoosh
Have you got a family?	**Tem filhos?** tehng feellyoosh
Would you like to see some photos of our house and our children?	**Quer ver umas fotografias da nossa casa e dos nossos filhos?** ker vehr oomash footoografeeash da nosa kahza ee doosh nosoosh feellyoosh
Are you going to the gala?	**Vai à festa?** vy ah feshta
Would you like to make up a party?	**Quer juntar-se ao nosso grupo?** ker zhoongtahr-sə ow nosoo groopoo
It has been so very nice to meet you.	**Gostei imenso de o conhecer.** gooshtay eemehngsoo də oo koonyəsehr
You have been very kind.	**Tem sido muito amável.** tehng seedoo mooeengtoo amahvel

Dating Someone

Are you on holiday?	**Está de férias?** əshtah de fereeash
Do you live here?	**Vive aqui?** veevə akee
Do you like this place?	**Gosta deste sítio?** goshta dehshtə seeteeoo
I've just arrived.	**Acabei de chegar.** akabay də shəgahr
What is there to do?	**O que é que há para fazer?** oo kə e kə ah para fazehr

I don't know anyone here.	**Não conheço ninguém aqui.** nowng koonyehsoo neenggayng akee
I'm with a group of students.	**Estou com um grupo de estudantes.** əshtaw kawng oong groopoo də əshtoodangtəsh
I'm travelling alone.	**Estou a viajar sòzinho(a)** əshtaw a veeazhahr sozeenyoo(a)
I'm on my way round Europe.	**Estou a viajar através da Europa.** əshtaw a veeazhahr atravesh da ehooropa
I come from Scotland/ Australia/New Zealand/the United States.	**Sou da Escócia/da Austrália/da Nova Zelândia/ dos Estados Unidos.** saw da əshkoseea/da owshtrahleea/danova zəlangdeea/doosh əshtahdoosh ooneedoosh
Do you mind if I try my Portuguese on you?	**Importa-se que pratique o meu português consigo?** eengporta-sə kə prateekə oo mehoo poortoogehsh kawngseegoo
My Portuguese is not very good.	**O meu portugués não é muito bom.** oo mehoo poortoogehsh nowng e mooeengtoo bawng
Would you like a drink?	**Quer beber alguma coisa?** ker bəbehr ahlgooma koyza
What are you doing this evening?	**O que é que faz hoje à noite?** oo kə e kə fahsh awzhə ah noytə
Would you like to go to a discotheque?	**Quer ir a uma boite?** ker eer a ooma boahtə
Would you like to join our party?	**Quer juntar-se ao nosso grupo?** ker zhoongtahr-sə ow nosoo groopoo
Do you like	**Gosta de** goshta də
dancing?	**dançar?** dangsahr
concerts?	**concertos?** kawngsehrtoosh

Do you like	**Gosta de**
	goshta də
the opera?	**ópera?**
	opera
the theatre?	**teatro?**
	teeahtroo

Can I walk along with you?	**Posso acompanhá-lo (-la)?**
	posoo akawngpanyah-loo (-la)

Which way are you going?	**Por onde é que vai?**
	poor awngde e kə vy

Do you mind if I sit here?	**Importa-se que me sente aqui?**
	eengporta-sə kə mə sehngtə akee

This is my friend, Tom.	**Este é o meu amigo Tom.**
	ehshtə e oo mehoo ameegoo Tom

Do you have a girl friend/boy friend?	**Tem uma namorada/um namorado?**
	tehng ooma namoorahda/oong namoorahdoo

We could make a foursome.	**Podiamos ir os quatro.**
	poodeeamoosh eer oosh kooahtroo

Do you play tennis/golf?	**Joga ténis/golfe?**
	zhoga tenees/golfə

Do you go swimming?	**Vai nadar?**
	vy nadahr

Which beach do you go to?	**A que praia é que vai?**
	a kə prya e kə vy

Would you like to come for a drive/a boat trip?	**Quer ir dar uma volta de carro/de barco?**
	ker veer dahr ooma volta də kahrroo/də bahrkoo

It would be nice if you would.	**Gostava muito que viesse.**
	gooshtahva mooeengtoo kə vee-esə

Thanks for coming out with me.	**Obrigado por ter saído comigo.**
	obreegahdoo poor tehr saeedoo koomeegoo

I enjoyed it.	**Gostei muito.** gooshtay mooeengtoo
Can we meet again?	**Podemo-nos voltar a ver?** poodehmoo-noosh voltahr a vehr
Cheerio! See you tomorrow.	**Adeus! Até amanhã.** adehoosh! ate ahmanyang
How about tomorrow?	**Que tal amanhã?** kə tahl amanyang
No, thanks. I'm busy.	**Não, obrigada. Estou ocupada.** nowng obreegahda. əshtaw okoopahda
Please stop bothering me.	**Por favor pare de me incomodar.** poor favawr parə də mə eengkoomoodahr

Mutual Interest

Do you play chess/cards?	**Joga xadrês/às cartas?** zhoga shadrehsh/ahsh kahrtash
Would you like to make a four at bridge?	**Quer ser o quarto parceiro para o bridge?** ker sehr oo kooahrtoo parsayroo para oo breedzhə
We play canasta/poker/whist.	**Jogamos canasta/poker/ whist.** zhoogamoosh kanahshta/pokər/whist
It is an English game.	**É um jogo inglês.** e oong zhawgoo eengglehsh
I'll ask the concierge if the hotel has a chess board.	**Vou perguntar ao porteiro se o hotel tem um xadrês.** vaw pərgoontahr ow poortayroo sə o otel tehng oong shadrehsh
This is	**Isto é** eeshtoo e
your king.	**o seu rei.** oo sehoo rray

This is	**Isto é**
	eeshtoo e
your queen.	**a sua rainha.**
	a sooa rraeenya
your knight.	**o seu cavalo.**
	oo sehoo kavahloo
your bishop.	**o seu bispo.**
	oo sehoo beeshpoo
your castle.	**a sua torre.**
	a sooa tawrrə
your pawn.	**o seu peão.**
	oo sehoo peeowng
We could play draughts or dominoes.	**Podiamos jogar às damas ou ao dominó.** poodeeamoosh zhoogahr ahsh damash aw ow domeeno
There is table tennis in the hotel. Would you care for a game?	**Há uma mesa de ping-pong no hotel. Quer jogar?** ah ooma mehza də peeng-pong noo otel. ker zhoogahr
Do you read English?	**Sabe ler inglês?** sahbə lehr eengglehsh
Would you like to borrow this book/this newspaper?	**Quer que eu lhé empreste este livro/este jornal?** ker kə ehoo llye ehngpreshtə ehshtə leevroo/ ehshtə zhoornahl

Conversations

There are certain universal subjects of conversation which provide a bridge for communication with strangers all over the world.

Among these are the weather, families, home, the cost of living and pets. The following conversational phrases are designed to start you off on an acquaintanceship with people who do not speak English.

About the Weather

It is a fine day.	**Está um dia bonito.** eshtah oong **dee**a boo**nee**too
It's not a very nice day.	**Não está bom tempo hoje.** nowng əshtah bawng **tehng**poo awzhə
Do you think it will rain all day/later/tomorrow?	**Acha que vai chover todo o dia/logo/amanhã?** ahsha kə vy shoo**vehr** tawdoo oo **dee**a/**log**oo/ahmanyang
It's going to be hot today.	**Vai estar calor hoje.** vy əshtahr kalawr awzhə
It's rather windy.	**Há bastante vento.** ah bash**tangt**ə **vehng**too
I think there is a thunderstorm coming.	**Acho que vem aí trovoada.** ahshoo kə vayng ahee troovoo**ah**da
Look at the lightning.	**Olhe para os relâmpagos.** ollyə para oosh rrə**lang**pagoosh
It will soon clear up.	**Daqui a pouco tempo pára.** dakee a pawkoo **tehng**poo pahra
We don't get this kind of weather at home.	**Não temos este tempo no nosso país.** nowng **teh**moosh **ehsht**ə **tehng**poo noo **nos**oo pa**eesh**
It's a pity it is so dull.	**É pena estar tão encoberto.** e **pehn**a əshtahr tawng ehng**koo**bertoo
Did you see the beautiful sunrise/sunset?	**Viu o lindo nascer do sol/pôr do sol?** veeoo oo **leeng**doo nash**sehr** doo sol/pawr doo sol
We had a very good/very poor summer last year.	**Tivemos um verão óptimo/péssimo no ano passado.** teeve**moosh** oong və**rowng** o**teem**oo/pe**seem**oo noo anoo pa**sah**doo

| There's a lot of haze about today. | **Está muito nevoeiro hoje.** |
| | əshtah mooeengtoo nəvooayroo awzhə |

| The atmosphere is very clear. | **Está um dia muito claro.** |
| | əshtah oong deea mooengtoo klahroo |

| Is it cold here in the winter? | **Aqui faz frio no inverno?** |
| | akee fahsh freeoo noo eengvernoo |

| I love the spring/ summer/autumn. | **Adoro a primavera/o verão/o outono.** |
| | adoroo a preemavera/oo vərowng/oo awtawnoo |

| What does the barometer say? | **O que é que diz o barómetro?** |
| | oo kə e kə deesh oo baromətroo |

Vocabulary

breeze	**o vento**	oo vehngtoo
cloudburst	**a trovoada**	a troovooahda
cloudy	**encoberto**	ehngkoobertoo
(to) drizzle	**chuviscar**	shooveeshkahr
dry	**seco**	sehkoo
forecast	**a previsão**	a prəveezowng
hail	**o granizo**	oo graneezoo
meteorological office	**o centro metereológico**	oo sehngtroo mətereeoolozheekoo
mist	**o nevoeiro**	oo nəvooayroo
pressure	**a pressão**	a prəsowng
rain	**a chuva**	a shoova
sleet	**a geada**	a zheeahda
snow	**a neve**	a nevə
sun	**o sol**	oo sol
temperature	**temperatura**	a tehngpəratoora
weather report	**o boletim metereológico**	oo booləteeng mətereeoolozheekoo

About Families

This is my wife/ husband/daughter/ son.

Esta é a minha mulher/o meu marido/a minha filha/o meu filho.
eshta e a meenya moollyer/oo mehoo mareedoo/a meenya feellya/oo mehoo feellyoo

My son is an architect/ doctor/student/ teacher/engineer.

O meu filho é arquitecto/médico/estudante/ professor/engenheiro.
o mehoo feellyoo e arkeetetoo/medeekoo/ əshtoodangtə/proofəsawr/ehngzhənyayroo

My daughter is at school.

A minha filha está na escola.
a meenya feellya əshtah na əshkola

She is taking her exams.

Está a fazer os exames.
əshtah a fazehr oosh eezaməsh

Then she will go

Depois vai
dəpoysh vy

to university.

para a universidade.
para a ooneevərseedahdə

to art school.

para as belas artes.
para ash belash ahrtəsh

to teacher's training college.

para um instituto de pedagogia.
para oong eengshteetootoo də pədagoozheea

She learnt some Portuguese at school.

Aprendeu português na escola.
aprehngdehoo poortoogehsh na əshkola

My wife is Scottish, but her mother is Portuguese.

A minha mulher é Escocêsa mas a mãe dela é portuguesa.
a meenya moollyer e əshkoosehza mash a mayng dela e poortoogehza

My father was a teacher.

O meu pai era professor.
oo mehoo py era proofəsawr

The children prefer to have holidays on their own.

Os meus filhos preferem passar as férias sòzinhos.
oosh mehoosh feellyoosh prəferayng pasahr ash fereeash sozeenyoosh

They prefer camping.	**Preferem acampar.**
	prəferayng akangpahr

My youngest/eldest son is married and lives in...

O meu filho mais novo/mais velho é casado e vive em...
oo mehoo feellyoo mysh nawvoo/ mysh vellyoo e kazahdoo ee veevə ayng

My youngest/eldest daughter is married and lives in...

A minha filha mais nova/mais velha é casada e vive em...
a meenya feellya mysh nova/mysh vellya e kazahda ee veevə ayng

Would you like to see some photos of our family?

Quer ver fotografias da nossa família?
ker vehr footoografeeash da nosa fameeleea

The younger children stayed at home with their grandparents.

As crianças mais novas ficaram em casa com os avós.
ash kreeangsash mysh novash feekahrang ayng kahza kawng oosh avosh

Are these your children?

Estes são os seus filhos?
eshtəsh sowng oosh sehoosh feellyoosh

The boy looks like his mother/father.

O rapaz [o moço] é parecido com a mãe/com o pai.
oo rrapahsh [oo mawsoo] e parəseedoo kawng a mayng/kawng oo py

The girl looks like her mother/father.

A rapariga [a moça] é parecida com a mãe/com o pai.
a rrapareega [a mawsa] e parəseeda kawng a mayng/kawng oo py

How old is he/she?

Quantos anos tem ele/ela?
kooangtoosh anoosh tehng ehlə/ela

My daughter is fourteen.

A minha filha tem catorze anos.
a meenya feellya tehng katawrzə anoosh

Vocabulary

aunt	**a tia**	a teea
birthday	**o dia de anos**	oo deea də anoosh
	[o aniversário]	[oo aneevərsahreeoo]
builder	**o pedreiro**	oo pədrayroo
computer expert	**o perito de**	oo pəreetoo də
	computador	kawngpootadawr
cousin	**o primo**	oo preemoo
daughter-in-law	**a nora**	a nora
divorce	**o divórcio**	oo deevorseeoo
father-in-law	**o sogro**	oo sawgroo
journalist	**o jornalista**	oo zhoornaleeshta
lawyer	**o advogado**	oo advoogahdoo
marriage	**o casamento**	oo kazamehngtoo
mother-in-law	**a sogra**	a sogra
relatives	**os parentes**	oosh parehngtəsh
salesman	**o vendedor**	oo vehngdədawr
technician	**o técnico**	oo tekneekoo
uncle	**o tio**	oo teeoo
wedding	**o casamento**	oo kazamehngtoo

About Homes

We have a house in the town/in the country.	**Temos uma casa na cidade/no campo.** tehmoosh ooma kahza na seedahdə/noo kangpoo
It is a detached house with two storeys.	**É uma casa independente de dois andares.** e ooma kahza eengdəpehngdehngtə də doysh angdahrəsh
It is	**É** e
a semi-detached house.	**uma casa geminada.** ooma kahza zhəmeenahda

It is	**É**
	e

a cottage.	**uma casa de campo pequena.**
	ooma kahza de kangpoo pəkehna
a maisonette.	**uma vivenda.**
	ooma veevehngda
a flat.	**um apartamento.**
	oong apartamehngtoo.

We have a large garden/a patio.	**Temos um jardim grande/um pátio.**
	tehmoosh oong zhardeeng grangdə/oong pahteeoo

There are two living rooms. One has a French window and the other a bay window.	**Há duas salas. Uma tem uma porta envidraçada e a outra tem uma varanda.**
	ah dooash sahlash. ooma tehng ooma porta ehngveedrasahda ee a awtra tehng ooma varangda

There is a fireplace in the dining room.	**Há uma lareira na casa de jantar.**
	ah ooma larayra na kahza də zhangtahr

The whole house is centrally heated/air-conditioned.	**A casa inteira tem chaufage/tem ar condicionado.**
	a kahza eengtayra tehng shawfahzhə/tehng ahr kawngdeeseeoonahdoo

We have two garages.	**Temos duas garagens.**
	tehmoosh dooash garahzhayngs

The back garden has a lawn and a swimming pool.	**O jardim de trás tem relvado e uma piscina.**
	oo zhardeeng də trahsh tehng rrelvahdoo ee ooma pəsheena

In our village there are many old houses.	**Na nossa aldeia há muitas casas antigas.**
	na nosa ahldaya ah mooeengtash kahzash angteegash

We prefer an old/a modern house.	**Preferimos uma casa antiga/moderna.**
	prəfəreemoosh ooma kahza angteega/mooderna

What kind of house have you got?	**Que género de casa é que tem?**
	kə zhenəroo də kahza e kə tehng

I like Portuguese houses.	**Gosto das casas portuguêsas.**
	goshtoo dash kahzash poortoogehzash

Do you cook by gas or electricity?	**Gozinha com gás ou electricidade?**	
	koozeenya kawng gahsh aw eeletrəseedahdə	

In a warm climate tiled floors are delightful.

Num clima quente é muito agradável ter chão de tijoleira.

noong kleema kehngtə e mooeengtoo agradahvel tehr showng də təzhoolayra

Wall-to-wall carpèting makes a house warm in winter.

As alcatifas aquecem a casa no inverno.

ash ahlkateefash akesayng a kahza noo eengvernoo

Built-in cupboards make a room seem larger.

Os armários de parede fazem os quartos parecerem maiores.

oosh ahrmahreeoosh də parehdə fahzayng oosh kooahrtoosh parəsehrayng myorəsh

Old furniture is lovely but very expensive.

As mobílias antigas são lindas mas muito caras.

ash moobeeleeash angteegash sowng leengdash mash mooeengtoo kahrash

VOCABULARY

balcony	**a varanda**	a varangda
bathroom	**a casa de banho**	a kahza de banyoo
	[o banheiro]	[oo banyayroo]
brick	**o tijolo**	oo təzhawloo
ceiling	**o tecto**	oo tetoo
chimney	**a chaminé**	a shameene
door	**a porta**	a porta
drains	**os esgotos**	oosh əshgotoosh
floor	**o chão**	oo showng
foundations	**as fundãnções**	ash foongdasoyngsh
gable	**a viga**	a veega
mains electricity	**a electricidade da companhia**	a eeletrəseedahdə da kawngpanyeea
gas	**o gás**	oo gahsh
water	**a água canalisada**	a ahgooa kanaleezahda
plumbing	**a canalisação**	a kanaleezasowng

stone	a pedra	a pedra
terrace	o terraço	oo tərrahsoo
tiles	os azulejos	oosh azoolayzhoosh
wallpaper	o papel de parede	oo papel də parehdə
window	a janela	a zhanela
window frame	os caixilhos	oosh kysheellyoosh
window pane	o vidro	oo veedroo
wood	a madeira	a madayra

Looking After Your Money

The Bank

Where is the nearest bank?
Onde é o banco mais próximo?
awngde e oo bangkoo mysh proseemoo

Do you accept traveller's cheques?
Aceitam traveller's cheques?
asaytang traveller's cheques

Can I use a Eurocheque card?
Posso utilizar um cartão Eurocheque?
posoo ootəleezahr oong kartowng ehooroshekə

Do you issue money against a credit card?
pode-se levantar dinheiro com um cartão de crédito?
podə-sə levangtahr dənyayroo kawng oong kartowng da credeetoo

I am expecting a remittance.
Estou à espera de uma transferencia.
əshtaw ah əshpera də ooma trangsfərehngseea

I have a letter of credit.
Tenho uma carta de crédito.
tehnyoo ooma kahrta de kredeetoo

I would like a draft to send away.
Queria mandar uma livrança para fora.
kereea mangdahr ooma leevrangsa para fora

What is the rate of exchange for the pound/dollar/Australian dollar?
Qual é a taxa de câmbio da libra/do dólar/do dólar australiano?
kooahl e a tahsha də kangbeeoo da leebra/doo dolar/doo dolar ahooshtraleeanoo

How much commission do you charge?
Quanto é a vossa comissão?
kooangtoo e a vosa komeesowng

I will have it all in 100 escudo notes.
Quero tudo em notas de cem escudos.
keroo toodoo ayng notash də sayng əshkoodoosh

Please give me 50 escudos worth of change.
Troca-me cinquenta escudos se faz favor.
troka-mə seengkooehngta əshkoodoosh sə fahsh favawr

Can you split this cheque into several currencies?	**Pode-me trocar este cheque em várias moedas estrangeiras?**	
	podə-mə trookahr ehshtə shekə ayng vahreeash mooedash əshtrangzhayrash	
I will have some Spanish pesetas, French francs and English pounds.	**Quero pesetas, francos franceses e libras inglesas.**	
	keroo pəzehtash, frangkoosh frangsehzəsh ee leebrash eengglehzash	
Can I open a temporary bank account?	**Posso abrir uma conta temporária?**	
	posoo abreer ooma kawngta tehngpoorahreea	
Can you arrange for some money to be sent from my bank in England?	**É possível mandar vir dinheiro da minha conta em Inglaterra?**	
	e pooseevel mangdahr veer denyayroo da meenya kawngta ayng eengglaterra	
I seem to be 50 escudos short. Can you please count it again?	**Parece-me que faltam cinquenta escudos. Podia voltar a contar se fazia favor?**	
	paresə-mə kə fahltang seengkooehngta əshkoodoosh. poodeea voltahr a kawngtahr sə fazeea favawr	
Have you a card showing current exchange rates?	**Tem uma lista com a taxa de cambio corrente?**	
	tehng ooma leeshta kawng a tahsha də kangbeeoo koorrehngtə	

Vocabulary

cashier	o caixa	oo kysha
cheque book	o livro de cheques	oo leevroo də shekəsh
coins	as moedas	ash mooedash
credit	o crédito	oo kredeetoo
debit	o débito	oo debeetoo
deposit slip	o talão de depósito	oo talowng də dəpozeetoo
foreign exchange regulations	a regulamentação cambial	a rəgoolamehngtasowng kangbeeahl
manager	o director	oo deeretawr

notes   **as notas**   ash notash
signature   **a assinatura**   a aseenatoora

Bureau de Change

Are you open outside banking hours?
Estão abertos fora do horário bancário?
əshtowng abertoosh fora doo orahreeoo bangkahreeoo

Does the rate of exchange alter outside normal hours?
Fora do horário bancário a taxa de câmbio altera?
fora doo orahreeoo bangkahreeoo a tahsha də kangbeeoo ahltera

Are you open on Sundays?
Estão abertos aos Domingos?
əshtowng abertoosh owsh doomeenggoosh

Can you show me your rates of exchange?
Pode-me mostrar a vossa taxa de cambio
podə-mə mooshtrahr a vosa tahsha də kangbeeoo?

Do you give the same rate for notes as for traveller's cheques?
Fazem o mesmo cambio para notas e para traveller's cheques?
fahzayng oo mehshmoo kangbeeoo para notash ee para traveller's cheques

On Losing Traveller's Cheques or Credit Cards

When this happens you should immediately notify the company that has issued the cheques or card but you may need help from a local hotelier or banker.

I have lost my traveller's cheques/ credit card.
Perdi os meus traveller's cheques/o meu cartão de crédito.
pərdee oosh meh'oosh traveller's cheques/oo mehoo kartowng də kredeetoo

May I ask them to communicate with me through you?
Posso dar-lhes o seu nome para que me possam contactar através de si?
posoo dahr-llyəsh oo sehoo nawmə para kə mə posang kawngtatahr atravesh de see

Have you a British
representative?

Tem um representante na Grã-Bretanha?
tehng oong rrəprəzehngtangtə na grang-brətanya

I hope they will be able
to replace the cheques
quickly. I have no
other money.

Espero que me consigam dar outro livro de
cheques rapidamente. Não tenho mais dinheiro.
əshperoo kə mə kawngseegang dahr awtroo leevroo de
shekəsh rrahpeedamehngtə. nowng tehnyoo mysh
dənyayroo

I will ask my bank at
home to send some
money to you.

Vou pedir ao meu banco em Inglaterra para vos
mandar dinheiro.
vaw pədeer ow mehoo bangkoo ayng eengglaterra para
voosh mangdahr denyayroo

Will you accept a
British cheque in
payment of the hotel
bill?

Aceitam um cheque inglês para pagar a conta do
hotel?
asaytang oong shekə eengglehsh para pagahr a kawngta
doo otel

Reference Section

Numbers

1	**um, uma**	oong, ooma
2	**dois, duas**	doysh, dooash
3	**três**	trehsh
4	**quatro**	kooahtroo
5	**cinco**	seengkoo
6	**seis**	saysh
7	**sete**	setə
8	**oito**	oytoo
9	**nove**	novə
10	**dez**	desh
11	**onze**	awngzə
12	**doze**	dawzə
13	**treze**	trehzə
14	**catorze**	katawrzə
15	**quinze**	keengzə
16	**dezasseis**	dəzasaysh
17	**dezassete**	dəzasetə
18	**dezoito**	dezaoytoo
19	**dezanove**	dəzanovə
20	**vinte**	veengtə
21	**vinte e um, e uma**	veengtə ee oong, ee ooma
22	**vinte e dois, e duas**	veengtə ee doysh, ee dooash
23	**vinte e três**	veengtə ee trehsh
24	**vinte e quatro**	veengtə ee kooahtroo
25	**vinte cinco**	veengtə seengkoo
26	**vinte seis**	veengtə saysh
27	**vinte sete**	veengtə setə
28	**vinte e oito**	veengtə ee oytoo
29	**vinte e nove**	veengtə ee novə
30	**trinta**	treengta
31	**trinta e um, e uma**	treengta ee oong, ee ooma
32	**trinta e dois, e duas**	treengta ee doysh, ee dooash
33	**trinta e três**	treengta ee trehsh

34	trinta e quatro	treengta ee kooahtroo
35	trinta e cinco	treengta ee seengkoo
36	trinta e seis	treengta ee saysh
37	trinta e sete	treengta ee setə
38	trinta e oito	treengta ee oytoo
39	trinta e nove	treengta ee novə
40	quarenta	kooarehngta
50	cinquenta	seengkooehngta
60	sessenta	səsehngta
70	setenta	sətehngta
80	oitenta	oytehngta
90	noventa	noovehngta
100	cem	sayng
101	cento e um	sehngtoo ee oong
110	cento e dez	sehngtoo ee desh
200	duzentos	doozehngtoosh
1000	mil	meel
1001	mil e um	meel ee oong
1100	mil e cem	meel ee sayng
2000	dois mil	doysh meel
100,000	cem mil	sayng meel
1,000,000	um milhão	oong meellyowng
first	primeiro	preemayroo
second	segundo	səgoongdoo
third	terceiro	tərsayroo
fourth	quarto	kooahrtoo
fifth	quinto	keengtoo
sixth	sexto	sayshtoo
seventh	sétimo	seteemoo
eighth	oitavo	oytahvoo
ninth	nono	nawnoo
tenth	décimo	deseemoo
once	uma vez	ooma vehsh
twice	duas vezes	dooash vehzəsh
three times	três vezes	trehsh vehzəsh
a half	meio	mayoo
a quarter	um quarto	oong kooahrtoo
a third	um terço	oong tehrsoo
an eighth	um oitavo	oong oytahvoo

| a pair | **um par** | oong pahr |
| a dozen | **uma dúzia** | ooma doozeea |

Time

Greenwich Mean Time	**G.M.T.** zheh emə teh	
Central European Time	**Hora da Europa Central** ora da ehooropa sehng**trahl**	
Atlantic Time	**Hora Atlântica** ora atlang**teeka**	
Date line	**Linha de mudança de data** leenya də moo**dang**sa də **dah**ta	
AM/PM	**da manhã/da noite** da manyang/da noytə	
24-hour clock	**horário de vinte e quatro horas.** orareeoo də veengtə ee kooahtroo orash	
summertime	**hora de verão** ora de vərowng	
12.15	**meio dia e quinze** mayoo deea ee keengzə	
12.20	**meio dia e vinte** mayoo deea ee veengtə	
12.30	**meio dia e meia** mayoo deea ee maya	
12.35	**vinte cinco para a uma** veengtə seengkoo para a ooma	
12.45	**um quarto para a uma** oong kooahrtoo para a ooma	
1.00	**uma hora** ooma ora	
midday	**meio dia** mayoo deea	midnight **meia noite** maya noytə

Phrases Referring to Time

What time is it?	**Que horas são?**	kə orash sowng
It is late.	**É tarde.**	e tahrdə
It is early.	**É cedo.**	e sehdoo
Are we on time?	**Estamos a horas?**	əshtamoosh a orash
At what time shall we meet?	**A que horas é que nos encontramos?**	a kə orash e kə noosh ehngkawngtramoosh
At what time are we expected?	**A que horas é que temos que lá estar?**	a kə orash e kə tehmoosh ke lah əshtahr
On the hour.	**De hora a hora.**	də ora a ora
By the minute.	**De minuto a minuto.**	də meenootoo a meenootoo
Every second.	**Cada segundo.**	kada səgoongdoo
At regular intervals.	**Em intervalos regulares.**	ayng eengtərvahloosh rrəgoolahrəsh
After the clock strikes.	**Depois do relógio marcar a hora.**	dəpoysh doo rəlozheeoo markahr a ora
Sunday	**Domingo**	doomeenggoo
Monday	**Segunda-feira**	segoongda fayra
Tuesday	**Terça-feira**	tehrsa fayra
Wednesday	**Quarta-feira**	kooahrta fayra
Thursday	**Quinta-feira**	keengta fayra
Friday	**Sexta-feira**	sayshta fayra
Saturday	**Sábado**	sahbadoo
daybreak	**o romper do dia**	oo rrawngpehr doo deea

dawn	**a madrugada**	a madroogahda
morning	**a manhã**	a manyang
afternoon	**a tarde**	a tahrdə
evening	**o fim de tarde**	oo feeng də tahrdə
night	**a noite**	a noytə
today	**hoje**	awzhə
yesterday	**ontem**	awngtayng
tomorrow	**amanhã**	ahmanyang
the day before yesterday	**anteontem**	angteeawngtayng

two days ago **há dois dias**
ah doysh deeash

the day after **depois de amanhã**
tomorrow dəpoysh də ahmanyang

the following day **o dia seguinte**
oo deea səgeengtə

weekday **o dia da semana**
oo deea da səmana

day off **o dia de folga**
oo deea de folga

birthday **o dia de anos**
oo deea de anoosh

Christmas Day **o dia de Natal**
oo deea də natahl

New Year's Day **o dia de Ano Novo**
oo deea də anoo nawvoo

All Saint's Day **o dia de todos os Santos**
oo deea de tawdoosh oosh sangtoosh

May Day (1st May) **o dia um de Maio**
oo deea oong də myoo

weekend **O fim de semana**
oo feeng də səmana

| last week | **a semana passada** |
| | a səmana pasahda |

| next week | **a próxima semana** |
| | a proseema səmana |

| for two weeks | **durante duas semanas** |
| | doorangtə dooash səmanash |

January	**Janeiro**	zhanayroo
February	**Fevereiro**	fəvərayroo
March	**Março**	mahrsoo
April	**Abril**	abreel
May	**Maio**	myoo
June	**Junho**	zhoonyoo
July	**Julho**	zhoollyoo
August	**Agosto**	agawshtoo
September	**Setembro**	setehngbroo
October	**Outubro**	awtoobroo
November	**Novembro**	noovehngbroo
December	**Dezembro**	dezehngbroo

| calendar month | **o mês de calendário** |
| | oo mehsh də kalehngdahreeoo |

| lunar month | **o mês lunar** |
| | oo mehsh loonahr |

| monthly | **mensal** |
| | mehngsahl |

| since January | **desde Janeiro** |
| | dehshdə zhanayroo |

| last month | **o mês passado** |
| | oo mehsh pasahdoo |

| next month | **o mês que vem** |
| | oo mehsh kə vayng |

| the month before | **o mês anterior** |
| | oo mehsh angtəreeawr |

the first of the month	o primeiro dia do mês	
	oo premayroo **deea** doo mehsh	
the first of March	**o dia um de Março**	
	oo deea oong də mahrsoo	
BC	**A.C. (Antes de Cristo)**	
	(angtəsh də **kreesht**oo)	
AD	**A.D. (Anno Domini)**	
	(anoo **domee**nee)	
Leap Year	**o ano bisexto**	
	oo anoo beesaysthtoo	
days	**os dias**	oosh **dee**ash
weeks	**as semanas**	ash səmanash
years	**os anos**	oosh anoosh
day by day	**dia a dia**	**dee**a a **dee**a
spring	**a primavera**	a preemavera
summer	**o verão**	oo verowng
autumn	**o outono**	oo awtawnoo
winter	**o inverno**	oo eengvernoo

Temperature Equivalents

FAHRENHEIT		CENTIGRADE
212	Boiling point	100
100		37.8
98.4	Body temperature	37
86		30
77		25
68		20
50		10
32	Freezing point	0
0		−17.8

To convert Fahrenheit to Centigrade subtract 32 and divide by 1·8. To convert Centigrade to Fahrenheit multiply by 1·8 and add 32.

Pressure

The barometer tells you the air pressure of the atmosphere. 15lb. per sq. in. is normal air pressure at sea level. This equals 1·06 kg. per sq. cm.

A tyre gauge tells you the pressure of your car tyres.

POUNDS PER SQUARE INCH	KILOGRAMS PER SQUARE CENTIMETRE
16	1·12
18	1·17
20	1·41
22	1·55
24	1·69
26	1·83
28	1·97

Measurements of Distance

One kilometre = 1000 metres = 0·62 miles

One hundred centimetres = 1 metre = 3·28 feet

One centimetre = 0·39 inches.

The following table gives equivalents for metres and feet. The figure in the centre column can stand for either feet or metres and the equivalent should then be read off in the appropriate column.

METRES	METRES AND FEET	FEET
0·30	1	3·28
0·61	2	6·56
0·91	3	9·84
1·12	4	13·12
1·52	5	16·40
1·83	6	19·69
2·13	7	22·97
2·44	8	26·25
2·74	9	29·53

3·05	10	32·81
3·35	11	36·09
3·66	12	39·37
3·96	13	42·65
4·27	14	45·93
4·57	15	49·21
4·88	16	52·49
5·18	17	55·77
5·49	18	59·06
5·79	19	62·34
6·10	20	65·62
7·62	25	82·02
15·24	50	164·04
22·86	75	246·06
30·48	100	328·08

MILES	MILES AND KILOMETRES	KILOMETRES
0·62	1	1·61
1·24	2	3·22
1·86	3	4·82
2·49	4	6·44
3·11	5	8·05
3·73	6	9·66
4·35	7	11·27
4·97	8	12·88
5·59	9	14·48
6·21	10	16·09
15·53	25	40·23
31·07	50	80·47
46·60	75	120·70
62·14	100	160·93

For motorists it is useful to remember that:

30 miles = 48·3 km.   70 km.   = 43·5 miles

70 miles = 112·7 km.   100 km. = 62·1 miles

To convert kilometres to miles, divide by 8 and multiply by 5.
To convert miles to kilometres, divide by 5 and multiply by 8.

Measurements of Quantity

Weight

POUNDS	POUNDS AND KILOGRAMS	KILOGRAMS
2·21	1	0·45
4·41	2	0·91
6·61	3	1·36
8·82	4	1·81
11·02	5	2·27
13·23	6	2·72
15·43	7	3·18
17·64	8	3·63

OUNCES	GRAMS
0·5	14·18
1	28·35
2	56·70
3	85·05
4	113·40
5	141·75
6	170·10
7	198·45
8 ($\frac{1}{2}$ lb.)	226·80
12	340·19
16 (1 lb.)	453·59

One kilogram = 1000 grams = 2·2 lb.

Half a kilogram = 500 grams = 1·1 lb.

When shopping for small items, it is useful to remember that 100 grams is about $3\frac{1}{2}$ ounces.

One metric ton = 1000 kilograms.

Liquid Measures

UK PINTS	UK PINTS AND LITRES	LITRES
1·76	1	0·57
3·52	2 (1 quart)	1·14
5·28	3	1·70
7·04	4	2·27
8·80	5	2·84
10·56	6	3·41
12·32	7	3·98
14·08	8 (1 gallon)	4·55
15·84	9	5·11
17·60	10	5·68

1 litre = 1·76 pints.

One tenth of a litre = 1 decilitre or ·18 of a pint.

One hundred litres = 1 hectolitre or 22 gallons.

One gallon = 4·55 litres.

One quart = 1·136 litres.

One pint = 0·57 litre.

Clothing Sizes

Measurements for clothes are made according to the metric system in Portugal and Brazil. Here are the sizes for the main articles of clothing.

Women

DRESSES AND SUITS

British	34	36	38	40	42	44	46
American	32	34	36	38	40	42	44
Continental	40	42	44	46	48	50	52

Men

SUITS

British and American	36	38	40	42	44	46
Continental	46	48	50	52	54	56

SHIRTS

British and American	14	14½	15	15½	16	16½	17
Continental	36	37	38	39	41	42	43

Index to Phrases